GOD QUESTIONS

By the same author

In the Steps of Timothy (Inter-Varsity Press, 1995)

What about it? (Scripture Union, 1996)

Storytelling (Scripture Union, 1997)

God
Questions

by

Lance Pierson

GODALMING
SURREY

THANK YOU ...

You can't make a good fist of being a Christian on your own. You need help from others. And the same's true of writing answers to 'God Questions'.

I couldn't possibly have written this book without the help of:

- Tom Agar, David Beales, Joan DeVal, Melanie Griffiths, Sean Gubb, Andrew Halloway, Adrian Levett, Kate Montagnon, Angi Shaw and Phil Sutcliffe, who advised on the format and the list of questions;

- David Allsop, Louise Aslett, Andrea Bent, Nigel Denton, Angie Edge, Andrew Killick, John McGinley, Chris Powell, Maurice Redmill, Timothy Reynolds, Nigel Styles and Howard Thompson with the lads and leaders of Guildford Crusaders, who read different parts of the book in its first draft and made invaluable comments;

- My friends in the Association of Christian Writers' West of London Area Group and Non-fiction Postal Workshop, who commented on several sections of the book as it took shape.

- Most invaluable of all were Alec Motyer who strove to keep me true to the Bible; and Lindsay Shaw, the patient and encouraging editor, who suggested helpful improvements to almost every page.

... AND SORRY

In the light of all they did, it's cheek to say that the book's 'by' me. It's really a joint effort.

But at least it means you should rightly blame me for anything you don't find helpful. It's my fault, not theirs. Let me say sorry for it in advance. Please talk it over with some other Christians who will help you find better 'God Answers' of your own.

To my own children, Joy and Robin,

my godsons David, Lance, Andrew and William

and to all new Christians —

WELCOME TO THE FAMILY!

CONTENTS

(continued overleaf)

5 GOD'S BOOK The Bible 113

6 GOD'S PEOPLE The Church 143

7 GOD'S PLANS The Future 165

GOOD QUESTIONS

WHO'S THIS BOOK FOR?

Not for your resident Bible quizmaster. It's for new(ish) Christians with plenty of 'God Questions' you want answered. Or with friends who ask those awkward questions about Christianity you wish you knew how to answer.

WHAT'S IT ABOUT?

One of Jesus' first followers was called Peter. He later became one of the leaders of the Christian Church, and he gave an instruction for all Christians to follow: "Be ready at all times to answer anyone who asks you to explain the hope you have in you".* This book tries to help: it gives answers to the God Questions so many people ask us.

They aren't just the answers Lance Pierson and his team of helpers thought up. They are all based on the Bible. That's the User's Guide God has given to Christians to help answer their questions.

With each Question you'll find a bit of the Bible quoted in full. And in the footnotes you'll find chapter and verse of other bits of the Bible you may want to look up if you're going into the question more fully.

HOW DO WE USE IT?

It's a handbook, not a bedtime read. The idea isn't to read it from cover to cover, but to look it up when you need help.

It groups the Questions in main sections (God's World, God himself, God's Son, etc.). Scanning the contents pages opposite should help you to locate the issues you are looking for.

The book gives the 'God Answers' one person and his helpers have found in God's Book. But the best answers for *you* will be the ones you find for yourself. So each section ends with a SO WHAT? list of *more* questions. They're there to help you come up with your own answers — and be ready to put them to use.

---

* 1 Peter 3:15.

Human beings are just an advanced kind of machine or animal

Why is the World such a mess?

What does God want us to do about the state of the Planet?

1

GOD'S WORLD

Humanity and other created beings

1.1 "What's the point of life?"

Meet Keith. Age 19. Average looks. Troupe of friends. Love life: what love life? Home: with Mum and Phil, his younger brother.

Follows the team on his free Saturdays. Plays a bit Sundays in the park. Twice weekly work-out at the multi-gym. Friday nights at the Three Bells, then on to the Eros nightclub, or take up a better offer on the party front. Home about 3a.m. — if at all.

Got a job at the local record store. Not bad. Pays the rent. Sample the new bands and CDs. Cheap tickets to some good gigs.

Lucky to have a job really. Especially one that lets him off every second Saturday.

Not sure where it's headed, and not bothered really. Might go up the ladder and become a manager. If they think he's that good. Not sure, really. But what else is there?

Pity Tracy left the shop. Fancied her. Fantastic hair. More than that, though. Good fun. Never let things get her down. Well, very seldom.

Sure of herself. Not cocky. Just secure. Didn't have to talk about herself the whole time. Like she didn't need to prove anything.

Never got round to going out with her. She seemed to be out every night. Loads of friends.

Good with the customers, too. Took an interest. Nothing too much trouble. Manager couldn't believe it when she left to go abroad.

He said she was some Bible basher, "on a mission from God". Pity about that. Makes you think, though.

THE POINT OF LIFE?

Keith says, "Not sure really." Tracy says, "Jesus."

Most people think like Keith. They seldom get round to thinking what life's *about*. But when they do, they don't look far beyond their own windows — work, friends, spare-time interests.

Many of today's leading thinkers push us right back indoors. They tell us to look inside ourselves to find the meaning. There are evening classes in self-discovery, self-realisation, self-improvement.

But Jesus points us beyond ourselves to something bigger and better. It's in *forgetting* ourselves and *giving* ourselves to a really worthwhile cause that we discover the point of life.[1]

That's what Tracy found. Following Jesus was a cause big enough to fulfil her. He is the one human being who has lived life to the fullest. His teaching and example can show us how it's done. His love for other people gave Tracy a reason for living that was more important than her pay packet and her job and her social life.

And believing in Jesus was a cause strong enough not to let her down. If things went wrong, she didn't collapse in a heap. She turned to Jesus for forgiveness and encouragement and a fresh start.

Even better — he's more than just a cause to live for. Christians believe he's a person to know and love. That he's still alive now for us to meet and share our lives with.[2] Not as a man on earth, of course. But as the God who made us and knows our true value.

God made each of us for a purpose. A one-off life-plan which only *we* can fulfil.

And he loves us so much, he wants to help us find that purpose in life and live it out to the full.

What Jesus said about the point of life:

I have come in order that you might have life — life in all its fullness.[3]

Love the Lord your God with all your heart, with all your soul, with all your mind, and with all your strength. Love your neighbour as you love yourself.[4]

If anyone wants to come with me, he must forget self, carry his cross, and follow me. For whoever wants to save his own life will lose it; but whoever loses his life for me and for the gospel will save it. Do people gain anything if they win the whole world but lose their life? Of course not![5]

---

1 You'll find what he said about this in the box of quotes from the Bible.
2 For more on Jesus being alive now, go to 3.7 "How can we believe Jesus came back to life from the dead?" (page 72).
3 John 10:10.
4 Mark 12:30,31. In giving this teaching, Jesus was quoting what God had said in Old Testament times. It is the truth for all generations. And note there is nothing necessarily wrong with loving yourself — provided you love your neighbour just as much!
5 Mark 8:34-36.

1.2 "Human beings are just an advanced kind of machine or animal."

Well yes, we're *like* machines in some ways. Starve us of fuel (food) and we run down. Use us in the wrong way and we *break* down. Program our minds and we are likely to think and act in the way you want.

We're even more like animals. We eat (like pigs), drink (like fish) and breed (some of us!) like rabbits. We work like beavers, sleep like dormice and die ... like fleas?

But that doesn't mean we're *just* machines or animals. Members of the same general type aren't all at the same level. An earthworm and a leopard are both animals. A penny-farthing bike and the latest pentium processor are both machines. But we're more struck by how they're different than by how they're the same!

A DIFFERENT SORT OF ANIMAL

Human beings are at the very least a different sort of animal or machine. We can think; we can train animals; we can design and construct machines. We have a sense of humour; a sense of beauty; a sense of right and wrong. Deep down, we know we *ought* to love and care for people in need, even if we don't find them attractive — and even if they live overseas and we've never met them.

We have a deep longing for life to make sense — to add up to more than just satisfying our animal appetites and mechanical reactions. We're spiritual beings with a hunger to get in touch with realities beyond the physical world.

The popularity of 'New Age' ideas is the living proof of this. High-street shops sell healing crystals, shaman's potions and books on Zen. Druids and spirit guides are back in business. Programmes and series with a supernatural edge always get good ratings.

Why? Because the 'god' of the 20th century Western world is dead. For two or three generations people have worshipped money and possessions. They're richer and more comfortable than their parents or grandparents. But they're no more fulfilled.

The reason is, we're not just bodies, minds and emotions. We also have a spirit or soul which no amount of money can satisfy. And that's the deepest part of our nature — our most important quality — the thing that really makes us human.

DIFFERENT *FROM* ANIMALS

Our spiritual nature makes us quite different from machines or animals. The Bible record of God creating the world makes this very point. It uses the word 'make' when it describes God adding another species of the same kind. "God *made* the sky, the sun, the moon" and so on. But it uses the word 'create' when he comes to a totally different kind of creature. "God *created* the universe ... God *created* all kinds of animal life ... God *created* human beings ... "[1] We are a separate order of creation.

Our spiritual nature makes us, in some respects, like God. He created us, as he put it himself, "in his own image"[2]. We're more like him than we're like animals or machines.

Of course we're not infinite like him. And we are no longer perfect like him.

But we are *people* like him. He made us to love each other and enjoy things. He made us to make things and look after his world. He made us to be good. He made us to know him and talk to him as his children and friends.

I don't know any machines or animals that can do all that.

$$\text{O LORD, ... you made them [humankind] inferior only to yourself; you crowned them with glory and honour. You appointed them rulers over everything you made; you placed them over all creation: sheep and cattle, and the wild animals too; the birds and the fish and the creatures in the seas.}^3$$

O LORD, ... you made them
[humankind] inferior only to
yourself;
you crowned them with glory
and honour.
You appointed them rulers over
everything you made;
you placed them over all
creation:
sheep and cattle, and the wild
animals too;
the birds and the fish
and the creatures in the seas.[3]

· · · · · · · · GOD

· · · · · · HUMANS

· · · · · · · · ANIMALS

LIFE INGREDIENTS
To make one human being you need:
● Enough fat for 7 bars of soap
● Enough iron for a medium-sized nail
● Enough sugar for 7 cups of tea
● Enough lime to whitewash a chicken shed
● Enough phosphorus to put the tips on 2200 matches
● Enough magnesium for a dose of salts
● Enough potash to explode a toy crane
● Enough sulphur to rid an average-sized dog of fleas
So what makes us think we're so valuable? *

1 Genesis 1:7,8,16; 1,21,24,27.
2 Genesis 1:27 New International Version.
3 Psalm 8:1,5-8.

* Adapted from David Watson, *In Search of God* (Falcon, 1974), p.40.

1.3 "Why are sex and relationships so important?"

What are almost all pop songs about? Love and sex.

What do men think about for an estimated average of 17 seconds in every minute? Sex!

What is the commonest topic of chat among women? Men!

What do most adults want most deeply in life? A partner.

Why are we like this?

Some people say it's because of the human race's need to keep itself going. Sex is the way to make sure there will be another generation. So we've evolved a strong drive for sex.

I don't know about you, but to me that seems to have missed a large part of the picture! God's explanation gets much closer to what it's really all about.

WHY GOD MADE US SEXUAL

Almost the first thing God says about us in the Bible is that he deliberately designed us in two sexes for love and friendship. Without friends we're lonely; we have no-one to talk to; no-one to share our lives with.

Of course, friends can be the same sex as us. And life's a whole lot richer when we share work or sport or interests with others who enjoy them.

But there's something special when we meet a friend of the other sex. Someone we fancy; someone we admire; someone we love. Someone we begin to want to spend the night with as well as the day. Someone we come to want to spend the rest of our lives with.

A SEXUAL GOD?

God didn't invent love and friendship just for humans. He feels them himself. He is a loving, friendly God. He says our sexual differences and attraction are a reflection of him.

> God created human beings, *making them to be like himself. He created them male and female ...*[1]

So we should squash the extraordinary idea that God is anti-sex or thinks it's dirty. He made it. He likes it. It gives us a feel of what he's like. Our sexual instincts and responses come from him. They are pure and beautiful and good.

But like all God's best gifts, they can be corrupted. The pressure of people round us can make us use sex the wrong way, or even worship it instead of God. That's why he takes the trouble to spell out what he designed it for.

SEX IS FOR MARRIAGE

God says he made us so we want to get together with a partner and stay with them forever. He's designed us to merge our singleness in a two-in-one partnership called marriage. As he sees it, each married couple is not two separate people any more, but one new family unit. *That's* what they're saying when they join their bodies together in making love.

So this is why he rules out one-night stands or prostitution or adultery. He's not trying to spoil our fun — but to save it! Anything less than marriage is much *less* fun, because it's trying to cheat the way God has made us. It's trying to have the marriage bed without building the bedroom and the rest of the house to go round it. Cheap — and very uncomfortable!

As for having kids and keeping the human race going, God doesn't say a lot about them — except that they're a good thing![2] But of course this lifelong two-in-one family called marriage is also the best way to bring up children; it's the safest, happiest home for them to be born and grow up in.

God said,

> It is not good for the man to live alone. I will make a suitable companion to help him.
>
> ... That is why a man leaves his father and mother and is united with his wife, and they become one.[3]

---

1 Genesis 1:27. For other things we can learn from this verse, go to 2.6 "Can we call God 'She'?" (page 44).

2 Genesis 1:28.

3 Genesis 2:18,24.

GOD'S WORLD

1.4 "You don't have to get married to live with someone."

Christians belong to Jesus and so we're committed to doing what he wants — even in our closest relationships.

That's not a sad or scary idea. He loves us, and the partner he chooses for us will be the perfect fit — the very *best* relationship we are capable of.

He calls that relationship marriage. And he says married couples are joined together — by God.

MARRIAGE — NOT A WEDDING

Jesus doesn't mean we have to have a church wedding with white dress, bridesmaids, etc. (though you're welcome to them if you or your parents can afford them). They didn't have a set wedding service in a synagogue in his day.

What he wants in a marriage is for you both to be 100% determined that you belong to each other and will stay together for the rest of your lives. That's a large part of what makes a couple married in God's sight.

One advantage of a wedding ceremony — whether in church or in a registry office — is the chance to make that promise to your partner (and in front of all your family and friends who will help you try to keep it). Just moving in together usually leaves it unsaid. Most couples living together as boyfriend-girlfriend start off giving it a try 'to see if it works'.

Tragically, in three cases out of four it doesn't. It breaks up in tears. *That's* what God hates, what he wants to prevent — the pain and bitterness of breaking up. He invented marriage to keep couples together and help them stay in love.

One pair out of four make it. They stay together. Many of them go on to get married publicly; and those who don't *are*, in a sense, 'married' privately. They remain faithful to each other for the rest of their lives. And that is what God wants for them.

But how much better to do it his way, and get married in the first place. All right, I know 33% of marriages end in divorce. That's 33% too many. But it's a whole lot less heartache than the 75% of unmarried partnerships that come unstuck. And couples who lived together before they married are 50% more likely to divorce than those who didn't. Living with uncertainty breeds insecurity.

THE BIT OF PAPER

Of course there's nothing magic about the marriage certificate. The security is not just in 'getting married', but in getting God's help with your married life.

The one in three divorces would be far fewer if couples went about marriage God's way. How many of them started really determined to make it work? And how many asked God's help when things began to get tough? He longs to give it. He's in the marriage maintenance and repair business.

Many people dismiss the 'bit of paper' as a meaningless contract between man and wife. Perhaps it's more helpful to look at it as a three-way deal: man, woman and God. At the human level, a lifelong pledge; and from God's angle, his service contract with a lifetime guarantee.

Jesus repeated God's words from Genesis:

> For this reason a man will leave his father and mother and unite with his wife, and the two will become one.

Then he added words of his own which show the incredibly high value he puts on marriage.

> So they are no longer two, but one. No human being then must separate what God has joined together.[1]

GOD'S WORLD

---

1   Mark 10:7-9.

1.5 "Why are Christians so against gay people? How can anyone live without sex?"

Gay people suffered gut-wrenching treatment from Christians for hundreds of years. They were mobbed, gaoled, tortured, even killed.

Christians did this because the Bible says God doesn't want people to have gay sex.[1] And probably because gay sex appears 'unnatural' in that it can't produce children in the way straight sex can. And, I guess, also because gay people are an easier target to punish than other groups who break God's laws, like liars or lusters.

There was no excuse for it. Jesus told his followers to be good neighbours to *everyone*, including gay people.[2]

He gives us the same orders. But we've still a long way to go in learning to understand anyone we know who's gay, to care for them and be friends with them. Many gay people feel that Christians condemn them and don't want to know them.

LOVE THE PERSON, HATE THE DEED

Gay people are human beings like everyone else. God wants us to respect and be good to them. But that doesn't mean we suddenly think gay sex is OK. God still says no to it — he even says he hates it[3] —because it is less than the best he wants for us. It misses the blessing he gives to straight sex. He makes a married man and woman into a new family. But he simply has not designed the human race (or the human body, come to that) for two men or two women to find this creative intimacy together.

The reason for gay feelings is probably not any so-called 'gay gene'. (Experts do not agree on the evidence for it.) The feelings much more likely stem from a damaged relationship with our same-sex parent early in life.[4] Later pressure in single-sex communities like prisons can exploit these feelings but probably not cause them in the first place.

The way forward is not a gay sexual relationship; but to find the *parent-love* that wasn't properly received in childhood. This can come from older Christians showing they accept us and like us as friends and equals. It can come from Christian friends who care about us and pray for us. It can lead to our sexual feelings gradually changing from gay to straight. I know this because it happened to me.

LIFE WITHOUT SEX?

It sounds tough, but it's not impossible. Despite the ideas the media put around, the sex act isn't something our bodies *must* do every day like eating or sleeping; it's part of what makes a marriage. And God promises to help people to live without gifts he hasn't given them for now.

One way he helps is to give love, support and happiness through a range of friends and relations. Another is to give us the inner strength to steer clear of wrong sexual fantasies, and the unhelpful 'friends', films or magazines that feed them.

I believe there's a third way, although not all Christians would agree with me. I've come to the conclusion that God allows many young adults, who would not otherwise be able to cope, to find relief in masturbation — giving themselves sexual release on their own. But of course they're not completely alone, because God is with them too. He loves us and understands us and longs to forgive us if we feel guilty. Many people find it difficult to keep their minds free of degrading fantasy. But in my experience God can help us be honest with him and fill our minds with simple gratitude, if we ask him.[5]

Jesus explained that there are many reasons why people can't be married and have a sexual relationship. But there's always a positive way to look at it. It's God's gift to them for *now*.

> This teaching does not apply to everyone, but only to those *to whom God has given it*. For there are different reasons why men cannot marry: some, because they were born that way; others, because men made them that way; and others do not marry for the sake of the Kingdom of heaven.[6]

Paul, Silas and Timothy gave this sex education to the new Christians in one of the first churches they started. Note that the Christians seem to have been able to live up to it!

> … you learnt from us how you should live in order to please God. This is, of course, how *you have been living* … God wants you to be holy[7] and completely free from sexual immorality. Each of you men should know how to live with his wife [or control his body][8] in a holy and honourable way, not with a lustful desire, like the heathen who do not know God.[9]

1 E.g. 1 Corinthians 6:9,10. Paul also mentions homosexuality in Romans 1:26,27, and this passage has led many Christians to treat it harshly. It is the first example Paul gives of the "filthy, shameful things" that people do in rebellion against God; and he dwells on it longer than any of the others. So some Christians have called it a worse sin than others. But this does not follow, and contradicts other parts of the Bible which condemn all sin as equally offensive to God. The reason why Paul mentions it first is probably that it was part of pagan worship which Paul has just been talking about in the verses before. It was also a very common, public practice in the first century Roman empire, with the emperor leading the way.

2 Mark 12:31.

3 Leviticus 18:22.

4 The evidence for this comes in two important books by Elizabeth Moberly: *Psychogenesis* (Routledge & Kegan Paul) and

Homosexuality: A New Christian Ethic (James Clarke), both published in 1983.

5 The Bible never mentions masturbation, so it is a subject we need to pray and make up our own minds about. But Jesus does condemn having sex fantasies about someone who is not your marriage partner (Matthew 5:28).

6 Matthew 19:11,12. Jesus' words sound a bit mysterious. I think he means: some people's characters are not suited to getting married; others have been put off it by something in their experience; while others stay single (at least for a time) to help their church or other Christian work.

7 "Holy" is a Bible word we don't often hear used in everyday life! Here it means 'completely free from sexual immorality'. But for a fuller understanding of it, go to 4.7 "How can I be sure the Holy Spirit's living in my life?" (page 98).

8 The Greek words mean either of these phrases — or both!

9 1 Thessalonians 4:1,3-5.

1.6 "Why's the world in such a mess? Isn't there *some*thing we can do about it?"

At college I met an overseas student. He was a Muslim from the country then called Yugoslavia. He longed and prayed for his country to be free from its Communist government and the control of Soviet Russia. I rejoiced with him in 1989-90 when suddenly his dreams came true.

But then they turned into a nightmare. His country split apart into Macedonia, Bosnia, Croatia and Serbia (with its beleaguered province Kosovo). And he and his fellow Muslims became victims of 'ethnic cleansing' — a revolting name for an even more revolting thing. They were exiled and even killed just because of their religion and race.

Why does this sort of thing keep happening?

You can point to various reasons which partly explain it. Like fear of people who look different from us or speak a different language. And the territorial instinct which wants a space where we can be sure of being free and safe. And greed to have more than we already possess.

But it's only the Bible which seems to me to get right to the root of the matter. It has an explanation *why* human beings are fearful, defensive and greedy.

PARADISE LOST

The Bible tells us of Adam and Eve (the original man and woman).[1] They lived in God's garden. God told them there was one tree they mustn't eat. But a snake came and sowed two poisoned ideas in their minds: (1) God was forbidding them to have something good; (2) he wouldn't carry out his threat that they'd die if they disobeyed him. Then they looked at the fruit and let it seduce them — it looked good, it would taste good, and surely it would *do* them good. So they broke God's law and ate the forbidden fruit.

You can't ignore God and get away with it. He checked that they'd deliberately done what they knew was wrong. Then he drove them out of his presence. They did not die *physically* there and then. But they *did* die a deeper, worse death. They fell out with each other and with their environment. But worst of all, they were shut out from knowing God as their maker and friend.

This restless, self-assertive, rebellious streak reproduces itself in every human being and every society. We all break God's laws when it suits us. This is what the Bible calls "sin". We not only commit actual sins time and again. But we have a permanent inbuilt tendency to sin. We're basically selfish.

So we suffer the penalty for sin. We don't naturally know God. He's so distant from us, we wonder if he's there at all. If and when we become aware of him, he's a frightening thought because deep down we all have a guilty conscience.

The world is so often a tragic and hostile place because it's the sum total of all our sin and guilt. People do *not* love their neighbours as themselves — either personally or nationally. We have a dim collective memory that things ought to be better in a perfect garden. But we can't make our way back into it.

That's no reason, of course, for not trying to bring peace and trust and understanding wherever we can. And the last ten years of the 20th century witnessed exciting progress in many of the world's trouble spots: between East and West, Arab and Israeli, the different races in South Africa, and even between Loyalist and Republican in Northern Ireland.

PARADISE REGAINED

But there's a deeper, more lasting peace on offer. As he died, Jesus suffered the punishment due to the whole human race for our rebellion against God. He experienced the total exclusion from God's presence which our sin deserved. So God now offers to make peace personally with any human being who surrenders to him.[2] He opens the gate back into the garden.

Then he fills that human being with his own love to go out and do everything possible to put right what's wrong in the world all around. The world will never be perfectly peaceful again in this life, because it's full of imperfect people. But an army of Christians dedicated to bringing the love of Jesus to bear on its problems can do a great deal.

And there's a whole new world coming one day. It really *will* be perfect.[3] Our job is to work towards it.

> So the LORD God sent him [the man] out of the Garden of Eden and made him cultivate the soil from which he had been formed.[4]
>
> … everyone has sinned and is far away from God's saving presence.[5]

> Where do all the fights and quarrels among you come from? They come from your desires for pleasure, which are constantly fighting within you. You want things, but you cannot have them, so you are ready to kill; you strongly desire things, but you cannot get them, so you quarrel and fight. You do not have what you want because you do not ask God for it. And when you ask, you do not receive it, because your motives are bad; you ask for things to use for your own pleasures.[6]

---

1 Genesis 3. Some people believe this story is more a parable than a historical event. The 'representative' names of the characters (Adam means mankind, and Eve life) lend support to this view; so does the talking snake. But that does not stop the story containing deep, God-given truth. They regard this as the story of the whole human race, just as Jesus' parable of the lost son is. Other Christians stress this must have been a historical event for the New Testament to make sense. It asserts that human history has been affected ever since these events. Jesus is the one who rescues us from Adam's devastating failure (see Romans 5:12-17). See also 5.10 "How do we know the Bible's true?" (page 134).

2 2 Corinthians 5:14-21. See also 3.9 "Why did God need to send his Son to die for us?" (page 77); and 3.12 "What does it mean to 'know' Jesus and have him in your life?" (page 82).

3 See 7.3 "What will heaven be like?" (page 170).

4 Genesis 3:23.

5 Romans 3:23.

6 James 4:1-3.

DANGEROUS

A prayer that dares to make the world a better place!

Lord, make me an instrument of your peace.
Where there is hatred, let me sow love,
Where there is injury, pardon,
Where there is doubt, faith,
Where there is despair, hope,
Where there is darkness, light,
Where there is sadness, joy.

O Divine Master, grant that I may not so much seek to be consoled as to console,
not so much to be understood as to understand,
not so much to be loved, as to love;
for it is in giving that we receive,
it is in pardoning that we are pardoned,
it is in dying, that we awake to eternal life.

– said to be by Francis of Assisi

1.7 "What does God want us to do about the state of the planet?"

The elephants were having a field day. Mice by the dozen crushed at every stride. The entire rodent civilisation was in peril — what could anyone do? "What can *I* do?" asked Minnie, "alone against such overwhelming forces!"

"THINK BIG," came the answer. Her whiskers twitched thoughtfully, then excitedly, then menacingly. "THINK BIG," she trumpeted, with a lash of her irresistible tail, and a thump of her thunderous paw.

A tiny elephant crept out of the floorboards to investigate the war cry. "Eek!" he squeaked. "It's Maxie Mouse." He turned trunk and fled into the rest of the herd.

Think positively and the problem shrinks to its proper size. THINK BIG is the key to coping with crises. And God's world is in a crisis.

It's dying of suffocation. Its atmosphere is poisoned and polluted. Its green areas are dwindling. Its temperature and blood-pressure go up and up.

Most Christians are so busy in their own fellowships or churches, they have never noticed the crisis in the world outside. Or if they have, they feel too powerless to do anything about it.

But this is God's world in God's universe. If we work with him, we can't possibly be powerless. THINK BIG. He can use our ideas to influence other people, form pressure groups, change public opinion.

He wants us to take in what he thinks about planet earth. That will help us see what he wants us to do.

BRING IT UNDER CONTROL

God's plan for the human race from the very beginning was "to live all over the earth and bring it under their control." He put us in charge of the animal and vegetable kingdoms.[1]

Some people have blamed God's words here for encouraging cruelty to animals and waste of the earth's resources. It's true that many modern processes for producing food and making things to sell have criminally damaged our environment. They've ripped the world up and hacked it down without any thought for the future. They've taken far more out than they've put back in. They've left little or nothing for the next generations.

But this is human selfishness and greed. It's not at all what God meant. When he says "bring it under control", he doesn't mean bleed it dry. He means the same as the instruction he gave the first man and woman in the Garden of Eden — "cultivate it and guard it"[2].

A garden's a good picture of the world and its resources. It's naturally fertile; it grows what we need to live on. But it's uncontrolled; if you leave it to grow wild, it will choke itself. It needs us to cultivate it, to get the best out of it.

But it's also vulnerable. It can all too easily be thrown off balance or even killed by exploitation and misuse. So it needs us to guard it from pests, disease, harmful climate and so on.

"Cultivate and guard" — that's what God wants us all to do. In the Old Testament he gave laws to protect the land from pollution and overuse.[3]

He may have given you personally very few of the world's resources — little more than a roof over your head and the clothes you stand up in. Or he may have given

1 Genesis 1:28,29.
2 Genesis 2:15.
3 Deuteronomy 23:12,13; Leviticus 25:1-5.

you comparative riches and power —
money, a house, a car, a job that
influences other people.

But whatever he *has* given you, he
wants you to cultivate and guard. Make
something of it. Care for it. Treat it with
respect. Make it last.

SHARE ITS CURSE

Sadly the world's no longer perfect. There
are obvious ways it's suffering from human
abuse — pollution, holes in the ozone layer,
exhaustion of fuels, extinction of species and
so on. The whole planet creaks and groans
with pain and frustration. When we look with
God's eyes at wasteful rubbish tips or the
effects of acid rain, or even litter mindlessly
carpeting the grass and clogging the rivers,
we want to weep and howl our protest.

But it's even more than these obvious
abuses. In a way we can't fully understand
or explain, we've knocked the whole
system out of the harmonious balance
God wanted it to have. We rebelled against
God; and because we were responsible for
the planet, we have forced it into hostility
against God.[1] At the same time it has
turned against us.

In Genesis, God describes three
symptoms of this 'fallen' world we now live
in.[2] (1) Hostility between human beings
and wild animals. (2) Trouble and pain in
pregnancy and childbirth. (3) Hard work
in making soil productive. Human
ingenuity can do a certain amount to ease
these difficulties. But God calls them a
curse which we can never completely tame
in this world.

HELP IT THROUGH PREGNANCY

But the New Testament sheds a brighter
light on all our environmental problems.
It's not a hopeless outlook which will never
get any better. God plans a new, perfect
earth in place of the present, flawed one.[3]
He looks on all the distress we face now
not primarily as signs of decay and
breakdown, but as labour pains. They're the
gestating embryo of the new order making
its first kicks and heaves.[4]

This is added reason for treating our
environment with gentleness and respect.
God didn't only create it in the past; he
means to re-create it in the future. He won't
thank us for a battered, tattered, shattered
old shell. He wants us to hand the earth
back to him, all the better for knowing us,
and ready for its new transformation.

In the meantime we should make efforts
to cultivate and guard — improve it and
cherish it.[5] If we apathetically let present
trends continue, we shall lose the lot. The
'elephants' will pound us to dust.

So God created human
beings, making them to be
like himself. He ... blessed
them, and said, "Have
many children, so that your
descendants will live all
over the earth and bring it
under their control. I am
putting you in charge of
the fish, the birds, and all
the wild animals."[6]

For creation was condemned to lose its purpose, not of its own will, but because God willed it to be so. Yet there was the hope that creation itself would one day be set free from its slavery to decay and would share the glorious freedom of the children of God. For we know that up to the present time all of creation groans with pain, like the pain of childbirth.[8]

God said:

Because of what you have done, the ground will be under a curse. You will have to work hard all your life to make it produce enough food for you. It will produce weeds and thorns, and you will have to eat wild plants.[7]

---

1 For more on our rebellion against God, go to 1.6 "Why's the world in such a mess?" (page 22). For more on why the environment is hostile, go to 2.8 "How can a God of love allow suffering?" (page 48).

2 Genesis 3:15-19.

3 Revelation 21:1. For more on the new earth, go to 7.3 "What will heaven be like?" (page 170).

4 Romans 8:19-23.

5 One good question people ask in the light of this is, "Should Christians be vegetarians?" It certainly looks as if the Garden of Eden was vegetarian (Genesis 2:16); and I respect anyone who eats no meat out of concern and care for the animal kingdom. But it's not compulsory for Christians. Paul says we're free to eat meat if we want to, as food that God has given us (1 Corinthians 10:25,26).

6 Genesis 1:27,28.

7 Genesis 3:17,18.

8 Romans 8:20-22.

1.8 "Is there a spirit world? Or is it all made up?"

The Bible says yes, there *is* a spirit world. It's all around us. Most of the time it's invisible and we're not aware of it. But at specially important moments, its inhabitants visit our world and make themselves known.

The chief inhabitant is God. He is spirit, not matter.[1] His natural realm is heaven, which is in a different dimension altogether from earth. And yet he made our world, and cares about it. He's forever trying to extend his love and values among the human beings he made to live on earth.

ANGELS

He's helped in this by the spirit beings who live in heaven with him. They're usually called angels. But you can forget all those Victorian pictures of sickly, sexless beings in choir robes. The Bible does once describe them as having wings — but six of them, not two![2] And when they appear on earth, although dressed in white, they look like *men*.[3]

Yet clearly they're not human beings. They're personal and intelligent like us (well, some of us!); but they're not limited to the physical conditions on earth. They're another race of God's creatures, acting as his servants and messengers.

They helped Jesus at critical moments in his life — when he was threatened with death as a young child, when he was tempted in the desert, and when he struggled to get himself ready to die on the cross.[4] And they appeared as a kind of heavenly commentary team on what Jesus' life meant. One angel announced that Jesus was going to be born; another (with full choral accompaniment) that he *had* been.[5] Others came to the disciples to explain about Jesus coming back to life after death, and then returning to heaven.[6]

SPIRITUAL HELP FOR US

Jesus talked as if the angels are interested and involved in our lives too. He said they rejoice every time someone becomes a Christian.[7] And they'll be there to take us to heaven when we die or at the end of the world.[8]

In a throwaway line that we don't fully understand, he said children (and perhaps all of us) have "angels in heaven".[9] This is a source for the idea that we have 'a guardian angel' looking after us. Most people dismiss this as about the same as a fairy godmother. But as the angels are God's servants, I certainly expect we get a lot of *invisible* help from them without even realising it.

Perhaps it's just as well this isn't absolutely clear. If people were sure they had guardian angels, I fear they might spend too much time thinking about them (even praying to them) instead of God.

God is the one really responsible for all the help we get. He could of course give it all to us direct, without making use of human or angel middlemen. But it seems he loves to share his work with others.

This is understandable enough with angels. But it's amazing God has the patience to go on making use of us, when we so often botch things or fluff our chances. Surely he could do the job of comforting people in distress or convincing them that Christianity's true much better on his own.

Surely he could. But he gives us our job to do and he trusts us with it.[10]

What are the angels, then? They are spirits who serve God and are sent by him to help those who are to receive salvation.[11]

1 John 4:24.
2 Isaiah 6:2.
3 E.g. Matthew 28:1-3.
4 Matthew 2:13; Mark 1:12,13; Luke 22:43.
5 Luke 1:26-38; 2:8-14.
6 Luke 24:1-7; Acts 1:10,11.
7 Luke 15:10.
8 Mark 13:27; Luke 16:22.
9 Matthew 18:10.
10 For more on the job God wants us to do, go to 4.9 "What are the 'gifts' of the Holy Spirit?" (page 103) or 6.2 "What do we go to church for?" (page 146).
11 Hebrews 1:14.

1.9 "Do the devil and evil spirits really exist?"

The Bible talks about them as if they really exist. They are not just picture language for the pressures and forces which make things go wrong.

The clearest and most convincing example of this is when Jesus was tempted in the desert. None of the disciples were with him, so they must have got the story from Jesus himself. His way of telling them what happened wasn't, "I was so hungry I felt tempted to conjure up some food"; it was "the Devil came ... and said ... and took ... then left"[1].

The Bible doesn't give us a full life-story of the devil. (A fact which itself warns us against getting too preoccupied in thinking about evil spiritual forces.) But it does tell us he was once one of God's brightest and best angels. Then he grew proud and rebelled against God. He was thrown out of heaven with a host of lesser spirits who support him.[2] But they're still active on earth until the end of time, when they'll be chucked on to the bonfire of history.[3]

GOD'S ENEMY

His usual name is Satan, which means 'enemy'. He and his army of evil spirits are totally anti-God. They're in there somewhere whenever there's opposition to God's will.

Occasionally this is spectacular evil or torment. Some people actually worship Satan or lay themselves open to be influenced, even oppressed, by evil spirits.

But most of the time Satan's plan is to stir up rebellion against God. He constantly 'tempts' people, Christians included; that's to say, he tries to persuade them to break God's laws. Then, if they're Christians, he plants nagging doubts in their minds: "You can't be much of a Christian if you do a thing like that. Perhaps it doesn't work after all." The name 'devil' means slanderer or accuser.

His cleverest tactic is to make most people (at least in the 'educated' West) think he's a primitive superstition who doesn't really exist; or a joke complete with horns and pitchfork. So they're off their guard against him. Yet those who do get interested in him he attacks quite viciously, even sometimes distorting their personality.

RESIST

The Bible has one word for what we should do about him — Resist!

When he tempts you to do wrong, say no. Have nothing to do with horoscopes, mediums, ouija boards, tarot cards or other occult practices, however harmless they may look at first sight.

When he makes you doubt or accuses you of being a failure as a Christian, ask Jesus to help you. Find some Christian friends or read something from the Bible. Jesus defeated Satan when he died on the cross and came back to life. So he can keep us safe and send the devil packing. But Satan tries to make us forget it.

If he really seems to be harming the life of someone you know, pray for them and tell Satan — in the name of Jesus — to get out. Better still, get some other, older Christians to pray with you.

But be wary of people who see evil spirits in anyone who's ill or has emotional problems. Human beings are complex creations who operate on many levels at once. To tell people all their problems are at the spiritual level is usually over-simplified. It can raise their hopes artificially that one prayer session will solve everything. And hopes falsely raised are cruelly dashed.

The best way to keep the devil at bay is, stick as close as you can to Jesus. When you're busy listening to him and doing what he wants, Satan will find it hard to catch your attention. The best way to beat evil is to do good.

In the Old Testament Moses taught the laws he had learnt from God.

> " ... don't let your people practise divination or look for omens or use spells or charms, and don't let them consult the spirits of the dead. The LORD your God hates people who do these disgusting things ... "[4]

In the New Testament Paul and James broaden the instruction out to cover all the devil's attacks.

> Don't give the Devil a chance.[5]
>
> Resist the Devil, and he will run away from you. Come near to God, and he will come near to you.[6]

1. Try writing a one-sentence "mission statement" for your own life. Begin it "The point of my life is to ..." or "I believe God has put me on earth to ...". Then rewrite it in the sort of words you would use to explain it to friends who are not Christians.
2. People often treat each other as if they were more than just machines or animals, even if they say they don't believe it. Think of some examples you have noticed recently. How could you point them out to friends who think there's no such thing as God or spirit?
3. How would you advise a single Christian who is the last remaining virgin among their circle of friends, and under great pressure to give it up?
4. What do you see as the pro's and con's of a Christian marrying someone who is not a Christian? Do you know of any Bible teaching about this?
5. Look at the information in the side-panel "Unmarried partners" on page 19. Which of the reasons do you sympathise with? Which do you think are just excuses? Why?
6. Make a list of practical ways you could help to cultivate and guard the planet better than you already are. Which of them could you start at once on your own? If the others need a larger group working together, who could you ask?
7. How far are you aware of Satan opposing God (a) in your life, (b) in the world around you? What would you recommend as three good ways to give him less of an advantage?

---

1 Matthew 4:1-11.
2 Revelation 12:7-9.
3 Revelation 20:10.
4 Deuteronomy 18:10-12.
5 Ephesians 4:27.
6 James 4:7,8.

Isn't God a crutch for wimps?

How do we know God exists?

How can a God of love allow suffering?

2
GOD HIMSELF

2.1 "Isn't God just a superstition for uneducated people, or a crutch for wimps?"

You can easily see how this idea got about.

"Once upon a time the sky lit up and rumbled. And people thought they must have offended the big invisible spirit who made it all. Or one of their number sickened and got no better. So they prayed to the 'gods' and she recovered.

But now we know about thunder and lightning and medicine and hygiene. So perhaps this invisible 'God' isn't there at all. Perhaps we just made him up to explain things we now understand better.

We used to hope we could go on living for ever. So we made up God to give us an afterlife in heaven. We long for protection and forgiveness; so we made up God to 'daddy' us.

But now let's throw off all this childish superstition. Let's be adults and face all our needs and anxieties alone without him."

WRONG PLACE TO START

The trouble with this kind of reasoning is that it only has a 50% chance of being right. If you can't see a God, it *may* be because he isn't there. But it may be because he *is* there — invisibly.

Take this alternative scenario:

"Towards the end of time people grew self-satisfied. They were pleased at how knowledgeable they had become and proud of all their scientific and technological achievements. They were comfortable in the hi-tech world they had built all around them.

Long-held ideas of a 'God' watching them and telling them what to do made them feel uneasy. The thought that they might meet him one day was threatening. So they were delighted when someone told them God might not exist. They quietly forgot all about him, and it suited them down to the ground."

We all have reasons for *wanting* God to exist — or *not* to exist. But that tells us nothing about whether he really does.

Trying to dismiss God as a crutch for immature people is just as fruitless. Of course it's possible that believing in an imaginary God would make insecure or neurotic people feel better. But as believing in him *does* help us feel forgiven and protected, it's equally possible that he's not imaginary at all.

The test of a crutch is whether it supports us when we need it. Christians claim God is 100% dependable. They don't mind admitting they're crippled — morally, spiritually, emotionally. We all are. We all need support of some kind at some time. How stupid to kick away the one prop that all its users recommend!

People imagine it's somehow more 'scientific' to think God's an outdated superstition. In fact, many scientists are Christians. In my University Christian Union, most of the members were scientists rather than people studying languages or history or economics.

Science is another false trail in trying to settle this question. It can only investigate the physical world around us. It can't tell us whether invisible, spiritual realities are there or not. It can't tell us everything.[1]

OK, a girl caught a fever from polluted water; and a course of drugs helped to cure her. But how do we know that's all that was going on? The doctor who treated her was a Christian, and he prayed for her. Who can prove his prayers to God didn't help as well?

RIGHT PLACE TO START

Starting with *our* ideas gets us nowhere. The different arguments cancel each other out.

If there's a book or a person that claims to know *God's* ideas, that's the place to start. And there's both — a book *and* a person. If they're right, that settles the question. God is no superstition; he's really there.[2]

In the past, God spoke to our ancestors many times and in many ways through the prophets, but in these last days he has spoken to us through his Son.[3]

We can find what the prophets said in the Bible. And God's "Son" is Jesus.

GOD HIMSELF

1 For more on the limitations of science, go to 2.3 "Hasn't evolution disproved God?" (page 38).

2 For more evidence that God exists, go to 2.2 "How do we know there's a God?" (page 36); 3.3 "Jesus was just a good man" (page 64); 5.5 "Why the Bible rather than any other books?" (page 122).

3 Hebrews 1:1,2. For more about the Bible, see section 5. For more about Jesus, see section 3.

"If God did not exist, we would have to invent him."

— Anon.

CREDO

"What?" they said, "Not God!
Not really! How can you?
A figment of mind,
A fragment of myth,
A projection …
And did you not know
He is dead?"

But they cannot tell me
Who answers me
Out of the darkness,
Or from where, beyond help,
Help comes.
They cannot tell me
The Name of my Friend.

There must be an answer,
For surely it is neither right
Nor reasonable that I, the foolish,
Should so confound the wise.

But I have launched a prayer
Into the vast spaces
And been swiftly heard.
I have prayed for a light
In the dark places
And a light has shone.
Lord, I have been foolish enough to believe Thy Word
And I have not been confounded.

Deep as eternity
Is the Rock my feet are set upon.

Evangeline Paterson

2.2 "How do we know there's a God? You can't prove he exists."

There are lots of things you can't prove. You can only reach 100% proof in maths or logic (or perhaps alcohol in a rather different sense!). But a lot of life has nothing to do with maths or logic.

I can't prove my wife loves me. But I don't lose sleep over it because there are plenty of hopeful signs. She agreed to spend the rest of her life sharing a house and a bed with me. She cooks for me, and washes and mends my clothes. She puts up with my dozens of irritating habits (including dividing up our life along such sexist lines!). And she *still* smiles and tells me she loves me and kisses me ... and more! She tells me her private thoughts and dreams — and she listens to mine.

What more 'proof' do I want?

EVIDENCE

I don't need proof, because in fact we all accept evidence that's beyond reasonable doubt.

We can't *see* the wind or radio waves or electricity. But we *believe* they're there — for goodness' sake, we *know* they're there — because of the evidence. Wind-socks, radio sets, electric power.

Same with God. You can't *prove* him, because that would make him a mathematical formula. Anything you can prove must be small enough for your mind to grasp. But the whole point about God (if he exists) is that he's *bigger* than us. He made us and lives outside us, on a bigger scale and dimension than us altogether. He's greater than our minds can take in at one grasp.

But there's plenty of evidence. I suppose it's theoretically *possible* that the universe with its uncountable variety of life-forms evolved from an original nothing. But I can't for the life of me see how.

Human beings have always tended naturally to ask, "*Who* thought that lot up?" Well, who? It's a reasonable question. It needs someone outside the universe to create something out of nothing.

And what about all the special good things in human life? Having friends; being able to enjoy music or sport; living by a set of ideals instead of basic instincts; caring for the sick and wounded even though they can give you nothing back. Why do these seem good ideas? Perhaps because there's Someone Good who designed them.

THE BEST EVIDENCE

There's much stronger evidence than anything we've looked at so far. A person. Called Jesus. He lived and died an unparalleled life. He never did anything wrong. He came back to life after he died. He said he was God in person. He was making God human — living him out in front of our eyes. The people who knew him best could only agree with him. God *is* real and alive — and living in Jesus Christ.[1]

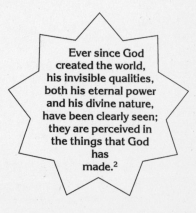

Ever since God created the world, his invisible qualities, both his eternal power and his divine nature, have been clearly seen; they are perceived in the things that God has made.[2]

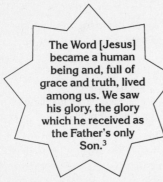

The Word [Jesus] became a human being and, full of grace and truth, lived among us. We saw his glory, the glory which he received as the Father's only Son.[3]

GENE DEFECT

Can evolution produce goodness? Richard Dawkins in *The Selfish Gene* writes:

"Much as we may wish to believe otherwise, universal love and the welfare of the species as a whole are concepts which simply do not make evolutionary sense."

Kindness and self-sacrifice hold development up. They reverse the process of evolution. So why do we call them good? To reach that idea of goodness you need God to create it and define it.

UNTITLED

We say there is no God
        (quite easily)
when amongst the curving
steel and glass of our own proud
   creations.

They will not argue.

Once we were told of a heaven
but the last time we strained to look up
we could see only skyscrapers
shaking their heads and smiling no.

The pavement is reality.

We say there is no God
        (quite easily)
when walking back through
Man's concreted achievements
but on reaching the park
our attention is distracted
by anthems of birds coming
from the greenery.
We find ourselves shouting
a little louder now because of the
   rushing streams.
Our voices are rained upon by the
   falling of leaves.

We should not take our arguments for
   walks like this.
The park has absolutely no manners.

                Steve Turner*

---

1 To look at this evidence more closely, go to 3.3 "Jesus was just a good man" (page 64).

2 Romans 1:20.

3 John 1:14.

* Steve Turner, *Up to Date* (Hodder and Stoughton 1983), p.22.

Evolution can't *disprove* anything.

Scientists and teachers often talk as if it's a totally established fact — almost a force or god. But evolution is only a theory. And like any other theory, it keeps updating and changing its details. Most people think it's a lot more certain than it really is.

But even if it was 100% certain, it wouldn't disprove *God*. For one thing, theories can't disprove facts. And for another, there's no clash between God and the idea of evolution. People only think there is because they've not been taught evolution, but what I call "Evolution with a capital E".

This is the double theory that (1) the universe evolved from simple beginnings to its present shape and (2) *it did so under its own impulse without any help from God who — by the way — doesn't exist.*

The bit in italics is a separate theory. It's in no way 'proved by' evolution, or automatically included in it. Evolution is simply the theory that the universe evolved in stages from simple beginnings to its present shape.

EVOLUTION OR CREATION

People say evolution clashes with the first chapter of the Bible, which gives its own version of how the universe began.

But what sort of version is it? Obviously it's hugely simplified. It would have to be, (a) to fit on to one page; and (b) to let people from hundreds of years BC onwards understand it. If it was in the latest scientific language, the vast majority of the human race through history would think it utter gibberish. And it would look absurdly dated in even ten years' time. Someone would have to keep rewriting the Bible.

But it doesn't try to be in scientific language at all. It talks of all the water under the sky being together in one place.[1] This isn't a geographical description of the oceans. It's an easy-to-understand listing of the different parts of the world as we know it: sky, water, land.

The short, clear story is telling us some vitally important things about the world we live in.

(1) God made it — it didn't happen by accident.

(2) He made it in a well-planned order — it isn't an irrational, unstable mishmash.

(3) He made it with a rhythm which still pulses through the whole thing — day follows night into weeks and seasons.

I don't see any clash between evolution and the idea that God created the universe. If the evolutionary stages happened, they could have been the orderly process God used as he worked.

This would mean that dinosaurs and other more primitive life-forms stalked the earth before us, just as scientific research suggests.[2] But they didn't just 'happen'; God made them while he looked after the world (in the same way that he does now).

SEVEN DAYS

Ah, but the Bible does talk of God making it all in seven days. Whereas evolution would suggest millions of years.

But what does the word 'day' mean in Genesis 1?

It may mean a single 24-hour unit. If so, it contradicts evolutionary theories. And if I as a Christian am forced to choose, I believe the Bible rather than a scientific theory.

Especially as it's something scientists can't study very precisely. This is partly because none of them was born at the time! And partly because, to form reliable theories, science needs processes that can be watched happening over and over again. This is difficult with the beginning of the world!

But the word 'day' in the Bible — and in everyday speech — doesn't always mean a 24-hour unit. Even in Genesis 1 it has different meanings; it twice means day*time* — day as opposed to night.[3]

But we — and the Bible — also talk about 'this day (and age)', to mean a long stretch of time. "How evil and godless are the people of this day!" said Jesus.[4]

More than this, Genesis 1 is telling us the story from God's point of view. And we learn from other parts of the Bible that "one day" can mean the same as a thousand years or more to God.[5]

So perhaps evolution is uncovering the way God went about his work. Genesis calls each stage a 'day' in God's week; but it was far longer than that on our time-scale. After all, according to Genesis, there was no sun to control the day's length till halfway through the process anyway![6]

THE HUMAN RACE

There's one other apparent clash between the Bible account and evolutionary theory as usually presented. That is the origin of human beings.

Evolution says we developed from more primitive forms of life. Genesis says God created us as a separate species with a unique resemblance to him.[7]

Again, I think there may be no real clash between the two versions. God could perfectly well take an evolving creature and change it into a human by giving it a spirit and other God-like qualities.

I readily admit, though, that not all Christians agree with this understanding.[8] It's an area where we need to be tolerant as we listen to other people's opinions and think about them carefully.

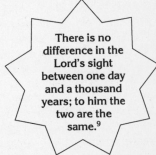

There is no difference in the Lord's sight between one day and a thousand years; to him the two are the same.[9]

So God created human beings, making them to be like himself.[10]

---

1 Genesis 1:9.
2 This is perfectly in tune with Genesis 1, where God makes animals before he makes humans (verses 24-27).
3 Verses 5,16. Compare Matthew 4:2. Indeed the word is more complex still. In Genesis 2:4 which sums up the creation story, the writer uses the word 'day' to cover the whole period of creation. Modern translations do not bring this out, presumably to avoid confusion. But the Revised Version of 1884 is completely accurate to translate, "These are the generations of the heaven and of the earth when they were created, in the *day* that the LORD God made earth and heaven."
4 Matthew 12:39.
5 Psalm 90:4; 2 Peter 3:8.
6 Verse 14.

7 Genesis 1:26,27.
8 One reason is the language of Genesis 2:7, "Then the LORD God took some soil from the ground and formed a man out of it; he breathed life-giving breath into his nostrils and the man began to live." You can certainly read this as a separate, later creation. I understand it as a more poetic alternative description to the earlier one in Genesis 1. It simply tells me that God created human beings out of the same matter as the world we live in.
9 2 Peter 3:8.
10 Genesis 1:27. For more on the special place of humanity in God's sight, see 1.2 "Human beings are just an advanced kind of machine or animal" (page 14).

2.4 "Aren't there some people you'll never persuade to believe in God? They're just not religious."

This is a common point of view. A reasonable one in an age when we're all encouraged to be ourselves. But I think there's a big fault-line in the idea behind it.

It imagines there's something called 'religiousness', which you're either born with or you're not. Just as some are born musical, but others are tone-deaf. Not a lot you can do about it.

But I very much doubt whether anyone's born **naturally** more believing or aware of God than anyone else. Of course, some are **brought up** by their family to know about the Christian faith (or any other faith, for that matter) and to treat it with love and respect; and others are not. But that's not having religion in your genes. They still have to choose for themselves whether to opt in or out.

In any case, Christians don't say to their friends, "Oh please be religious. Do try a bit harder to believe in God." That's not what Christianity is about.

What we say is, There **is** a God, whether you believe in him or not. He made himself perfectly clear in the life and actions of Jesus. If you didn't realise it was so clear, get hold of one of the Gospels and read it with an open mind.[1] He challenges you to check out his claims for yourself.

If you give it a fair trial, you'll know.

Jesus says *he* is the whole truth about life.[3] If you ignore him and try to live your life without a God-dimension, you're missing the truth. You're building your life on a fantasy which will collapse under you at any moment.

You may not *feel* in any danger. You may not *feel* 'religious' or as if there's a God. But the *fact* is, Jesus said he was God; said he would come back to life after he died; and he would then return to earth to judge people's lives when they least expected it.

Many people say their teeth *feel* OK, so they don't need to go to the dentist. But they're in for a nasty shock if they've got their *facts* wrong. It makes sense to check.

It's the same with Jesus. It's unbelievably stupid not to check. If he's got his facts right, there's a date already set when he will ask you why you haven't made peace with your Maker. It will be too late then to say, "I didn't feel religious."

Right now, though, he says, "Come to me. I'll show you the true facts about life which you are missing out on." When you do, you'll wonder why on earth you left it so long.

Words of wisdom from King David who knew God well.

> What I teach is not my own teaching, but it comes from God, who sent me. Whoever is willing to do what God wants will know whether what I teach comes from God or whether I speak on my own authority.[2]

> Fools say to themselves, "There is no God."[4]

This was St Paul's message to people in Athens who were not Christians:

God has overlooked the times when people did not know him, but now he commands all of them everywhere to turn away from their evil ways. For he has fixed a day in which he will judge the whole world with justice by means of a man he has chosen. He has given proof of this to everyone by raising that man from death![5]

1 See section 3 for fuller information on these facts about Jesus.
2 John 7:16,17.
3 John 14:6.
4 Psalm 14:1.
5 Acts 17:30,31.

It would be hard to take the gods of ancient Rome and Greece seriously today. They were much too like us. They warred and whored and cheated and lied like the worst of us. Not exactly your dream team to run the universe.

The eastern religions are quite the opposite. God, if there at all, is totally unlike us. 'He' (or It) verges on the unknowable. The divine spirit is a mystic life-force at the heart of all being — or in each of us. One Christian teacher has said this makes God sound rather like a cosmic rice pudding.

A PERSON

The Bible steers a middle course. God, it says, is **morally** different from us. He's perfectly just, right and good. But in one vital part of his nature, he **is** like us: he's personal.

This doesn't mean he's physical, with a body, arms and legs. But it means he thinks, plans and decides. He wants and feels, loves and hates. He does things and makes himself known.

It also means we can relate to him. He speaks to us in language we can understand. And we can talk back to him.

He showed all this most clearly in Jesus. God came to earth and lived as a **person**. He shared our human personality in every way — except that he did nothing wrong.[1]

A FATHER

When people asked to know what God was like, Jesus told them to look at **him**.[2] But he also used a name for God which perhaps tells us all we want to know. He called him Father. God is not 'the Force', but 'the Father'.

Some people find this idea frightening at first (or at best meaningless), because they had bad fathers, or never knew who their dad was. But God's a perfect Father, as in the 'Our Father' prayer Jesus taught his followers to pray.[3]

(1) The opening note is God's **authority**. "May your holy name be honoured." Fathers in the ancient world had the power of life and death over their children. They expected instant obedience. But God's higher up than our human father; he's our Father in heaven. His name and his whole being are holy — sacred and pure.[4] You can't mess around with him.

(2) Then the prayer moves on to God's fatherly **care**. "Give us today the food we need" — he provides for us. "Keep us safe from the Evil One" — he protects us. And he does both generously, because he's everything a father should be. Jesus went on to drum this point in. "Bad as you are, you know how to give good things to your children. How much more, then, will your Father in heaven give good things to those who ask him!"[5]

(3) The prayer leads us finally into God's merciful **love**. "Forgive us the wrongs we have done." Jesus' most famous teaching about God as Father is the story of the Lost Son, who throws away his inheritance and expects to have to earn his way back into his father's household. He finds himself hugged, kissed, celebrated, given the place of honour.[6] That's how God loves all of us.

The Lord's Prayer teaches us to talk to God with the polite and formal name 'Father'. But Jesus called him 'Abba' — the word in his Aramaic language for Dad. And Paul teaches that the Holy Spirit leads us too to call God 'Abba' or 'Dad'.[7] That's how close and intimate God wants the relationship to be.

Some people have imagined that God is somehow the Father of the whole human race. But that's not what the New Testament is saying. The Lord's Prayer is for Christians. Jesus only gives the title-deeds to God's family to "whoever does what God wants him to do".[8] Paul explains that the Holy Spirit makes us God's children only when we become followers of Jesus.[9]

God would *love* the whole human race to become his children. It's up to us to tell them how to join the family.

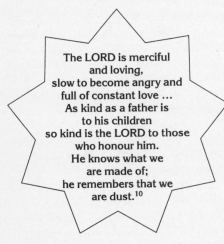

The LORD is merciful
and loving,
slow to become angry and
full of constant love ...
As kind as a father is
to his children
so kind is the LORD to those
who honour him.
He knows what we
are made of;
he remembers that we
are dust.[10]

---

1. Hebrews 2:14; 4:15. See also 3.3 "Jesus was just a good man" (page 64).
2. John 14:9.
3. Matthew 6:9-13.
4. For more on what 'holy' means, go to 4.7 "How can I be sure the Holy Spirit's living in my life?" (page 98). And for more on God's holiness, go to 7.4 "Won't everyone go to heaven?" (page 172).
5. Matthew 7:11.
6. Luke 15:11-24.
7. This is the word he uses in Romans 8:15.
8. Mark 3:35.
9. Romans 8:1,2; 14-16.
10. Psalm 103:8,13,14.

THE LORD'S PRAYER
Our Father in heaven,
hallowed be your name,
your kingdom come,
your will be done,
on earth as in heaven.
Give us today our daily bread.
Forgive us our sins
as we forgive those who sin against us.
Lead us not into temptation
but deliver us from evil.
For the kingdom, the power, and the
  glory are yours
now and for ever. Amen.

A TO Z
David Pawson preached a series of sermons on God's character. He based the titles on the letters of the alphabet. They make a brilliantly memorable summary.

1. Almighty Bountiful Creator
2. Deity and Eternity
3. Fatherly Goodness
4. Holiness, Indignation, Justice
5. Kindness, Love, Mercy
6. Names of God (used in the Bible)
7. Order, Peace, Quiet
8. Reign and Sovereignty
9. Trinity and Unity
10. Vengeance and Wrath
11. 'X marks the spot' — God's character revealed in Jesus and his death, fulfilling two Old Testament concepts, the Year of the Lord and the Zeal of the Lord.

2.6 "Can we call God 'She'?"

In the early days of political correctness there was a joke about God. A famous preacher made it to heaven and got a severe shock. "I saw God," he spluttered. "And she's *black*!"

The joke was that he took in his stride the seemingly more preposterous idea — that God was female.

But now people ask, why not?

The feminist movement has rightly challenged every male chauvinist idea it can sniff out. If male and female are equally good (and they are), why do we have to call God 'he'?[1]

GOD THE MOTHER?

Well, the Bible does occasionally describe God in female language. Jesus compared himself to a mother-hen gathering her chicks under her wings.[2] And God promised through the prophet Isaiah that he would comfort his people "as a mother comforts her child".[3]

Even more important is the Bible saying that when God made human beings to be like himself, he created them male *and female*.[4] When the Bible uses male language about God, it doesn't mean he's a non-female or he can't understand girls and women. He made them as much in his own image as men and boys are.

He's greater than human gender differences. He has what have been traditionally thought of as 'female' qualities (such as gentleness and sensitivity) as well as 'male' ones (e.g. strength and logical reasoning!). Only the full range of human personality — female and male together —can reflect what God's like. Moses had a brilliant insight when he told the Old Testament people that God *both* "fathered" them *and* "gave them birth" (ie. mothered them).[5] And when David says God is "as kind as a father is to his children", the word "kind" means mother-love; it's first cousin to the word "womb"![6] In his fatherliness, God loves us like a mother.

So I reckon it's OK to think of God as Mum — especially in your own prayers — if that's what's most helpful to you. I think it's OK to talk about him as 'our Parent' if you or the person you're talking to have bad experiences of dads.

GOD THE FATHER

But Jesus always called God his (or the) Father. And the Bible always calls 'him'(!) 'he' in the original language, even though it sometimes uses feminine words to describe him. This is so constant and on such high authority that I think it's more than just the way people thought at that time; it's the way God wants us to understand him. So I would like English Bibles to go on translating with the male form. And I think we should follow Jesus in referring to God as 'he' in our praise and prayer sessions.

My human father left my mum and me when I was one; I never met him till I was 33. So I grew up with a painful and secondhand picture of dads. But that didn't stop me understanding God as the perfect and totally reliable Father who would never desert me.

And I believe part of the job of Christian men today is to give children and young people a feel of what God-like dads should be. They should give us an image of what God is like.

So God created
human beings,
making them to be
like himself. He
created them male
and female …[7]

This, then,
is how you
should pray:

"Our Father … "[8]

---

1   For comments on sexist language in the Bible,
    go to 5.9 "Hasn't the Bible been changed over
    the years?" (page 132). Another attack on
    tradition comes from the poor image of
    fatherhood these days: see 2.5 "What's God
    like?" (page 42).

2   Luke 13:34.

3   Isaiah 66:13.

4   Genesis 1:27.

5   Deuteronomy 32:18 New International
    Version.

6   Psalm 103:13.

7   Genesis 1:27.

8   Matthew 6:9.

2.7 "How can God know all about us— and be interested in all of us?"

Robin had problems with one of his computer games. The instructions didn't tell him enough to sort it out. And the shop couldn't help. But through a magazine, he found the phone number of the game's designer. Rather nervously his dad (that's me!) rang him up and asked if he would be kind enough to help. He said he'd be delighted, and he talked us through the difficulties to a solution. He'd thought the game up, so he knew it inside out.

MAKER

God designed *us*. We are his idea and invention. He knows exactly how we tick because he made us.

And of course we're not all mass-produced, identical clones. God loves variety and he made us all different. Each of us has a different shape, different finger-prints, and a different personality. And because God's *infinitely* brilliant, he knows every one of us equally well.

What's more, he's *been* one of us. As Jesus, he was the creature as well as the Creator. He knows human life from the inside. He understands our feelings, moods, fears, hopes, dreams, loves. He's had them himself. He still does, for Jesus took them back to heaven with him as part of his human nature.

But although he loves more deeply than any mere human, he's got no favourites. He loves each of us equally.

MINDER

He's not just the maker; he's also the maintainer. It's as if he's got a service contract on each of us. He takes a loving interest in the happiness and welfare of every single one.

I once read a book where the cook in a Christian community described her job. She didn't just dole out chicken casserole for 50. She knew the special diet of each person and kept them all in mind as she prepared. This one's a vegetarian; that one's on a low-fat regime; she can't eat eggs; he doesn't like onions; and so on. God is the master chef who meets *all* our special needs.

But he doesn't meet us only at set mealtimes. And he doesn't just sit in the office waiting for an emergency call. He looks after us all the time — even when we're asleep and can't look after ourselves. He's got eyes everywhere — able to watch every single person for every single moment of every day. He's a bit like those security cameras in supermarkets. Except he's with us wherever we go; and he can see right inside us to the thoughts, as well as the outside actions and words.

Ouch! Bad news for our less commendable moments. I know *my* thoughts, words and deeds aren't always a pretty sight. And if they make me wince, they must hurt God even more. We need to keep saying sorry to him as well as asking for his help. If *we* were God, I'm convinced we'd give ourselves up as a bad job.

But here's a saying that has helped me time and again. *God knows the worst about us, yet he loves us all the same.* He loves us in spite of our faults and failures. He loves us enough to want to help us put them right. He loves us enough to want to make us his children.[1]

That's some love. Some God!

Some words about God by David:

> He is good to
> everyone
> and has compassion
> on all he made ...
> He helps those who
> are in trouble;
> he lifts those who
> have fallen.[2]

When Peter saw God letting Gentiles as well as Jews become Christians, he said:

> I now realize
> that it is true
> that God treats
> everyone on
> the same
> basis.[3]

---

1 1 John 3:1.
2 Psalm 145:9,14.
3 Acts 10:34.

2.8 "How can a God of love allow suffering?"

Night after night we see them in close-up. Families numbed or choking on tears because a loved one has been shot, burnt or bombed out of this world … children disfigured by hunger or disease … How can God allow these outrages to happen?

Sometimes the question comes right home to our own door. A close friend or relation dies … our parents split up … we have a terrible accident … our hopes are crushed. The pain is unbearable. What on earth is God doing?

We were told God is infinitely powerful and infinitely loving. So surely he should stop all this suffering?

Undoubtedly he *could*. But is this really what we want? And would it be the best thing for us?

YOU CAN'T BLAME GOD

The vast majority of suffering in the world — someone calculated about 95% — is 'man-made'. We can't blame God for every terrible incident of human crime and cruelty.

There's more than enough food in the world to feed every hungry mouth; but we in the overfed nations hoard it for ourselves while we blame God for letting children starve.

What do we expect God to do? Miraculously transplant the butter-mountains and wine-lakes from Europe to Africa? Force the European Parliament like robots to debate the question and reach the right decision? But that's what he expects *us* to do. He's put us in charge of the world's resources. It's our human responsibility to arrange a fair distribution.

In the same way, is he supposed suddenly to jam the brakes of the drunken driver about to hit another car? Or whisk away the girl on the point of being raped? If he did, you can be quite certain the very

people who blame him for all the suffering in the world would criticise him for interfering and treating us as less than human. And this time they would be right.

Think what it would do to us if we thought God would always step in and stop anyone getting hurt. We would become even more selfish and thoughtless than we are already. There'd be no need to look out for others — that would be God's department. We could smash, grab, lie, steal and kill to our heart's content — and no-one else would feel a thing.

But in the real world God has made, cars do crash and violence does hurt. And that's a good thing. It's one of God's ways to teach us to live responsibly — to respect and care for other people. This is one thing that makes us different from machines or animals. We can choose to control our lust for drink or sex — or anything else that would hurt others.

WHO CAN YOU BLAME?

But what about other kinds of suffering which humans don't cause — like earthquakes and unpreventable illness? Granted, we don't deliberately create hurricanes or plagues. But a great many natural disasters are made far worse by human selfishness and greed. Destruction of the environment for quick profits has upset the balance of nature — poisoned waterways and farmland, soil erosion, acid rain and exposure to harmful sunrays are some of the results.

And the terrible scourge of AIDS has only spread so widely because people think they know better than God about sex. Some people have caught HIV through drug abuse or blood transfusions; but the vast majority through having sex with an infected partner. God's simple rule that we should stick to one sex partner for life is the only way to *really* safe sex. It makes us immune to that way of getting AIDS.

But that still doesn't explain *why* natural disasters happen in the first place. And we don't fully understand the explanation the Bible gives us.

It simply says God made the human race responsible for the whole planet. So when we rebelled against him, we dragged the world down with us. We damaged it and made it hostile.

Then God said, "And now we will make human beings ... They will have power over the fish, the birds, and all animals ... " "Because of what you have done, the ground will be under a curse ... It will produce weeds and thorns, and you will have to eat wild plants."[1]

There's no *direct* link between wrong things I've done and the amount I suffer in life. I don't develop cancer *because* I walked out on my parents or fiddled the books at work. But my self-centredness adds to the world's struggles and disintegration. It has fallen out of the groove God built it for. And my wrongdoing was part of the dead weight that pulled it down.

BEYOND BLAME

Much is uncertain, but three things about God we know for sure.

(1) He doesn't want all this pain and suffering. It hurts him even more than it hurts us. He tells his people to comfort those who suffer and do all they can to cut down the sum of human misery. He plans a bright future for us in the next life when there will be no more crying or pain.

And we shall then see that the strains and stresses of life on earth were a very light affliction compared with the glory to come.[2]

(2) He doesn't cut himself off from the pain. He feels every ache and pang. And he's been through even worse himself. He came as Jesus to suffer. To die one of the most revolting death penalties that human cruelty has devised. And more than that, to go through the depths of hell that every one of us deserves — to rescue us from any form of suffering in the next life. *That* is the resolute, shatter-proof, unending love of God for us.

(3) He can bring good out of (or into) the suffering. He turns it from a curse into a blessing. He doesn't leave us to face it alone, but stays with us as our 24-hour care assistant. He helps us learn and grow in a way that we never would if life was all sunshine. So Jesus turns our usual way of looking at things upside down, saying that poverty, hunger and tears are blessings, while wealth, satisfaction and laughter are woes![3]

The Old Testament says a lot about God's reaction to suffering.

He does not neglect the poor or ignore their suffering;
he does not turn away from them,
but answers when they call for help.[4]

The prophet Isaiah forecasts Jesus' suffering with quite extraordinary insight.
We despised him and rejected him;
he endured suffering and pain.
No one would even look at him —
we ignored him as if he were
nothing.

(continued overleaf)

---

1 Genesis 1:26; 3:17,18.
2 Luke 10:27-37; Revelation 21:4; Romans 8:18.
3 Luke 6:20-26.
4 Psalm 22:24.

2.9 "Why does religion cause wars and division?"

But he endured the suffering
that should have been ours,
the pain that we should have borne.
All the while we thought that his
suffering was punishment sent by God.
But because of our sins he was
wounded,
beaten because of the evil we did.
We are healed by the punishment
he suffered, made whole by the
blows he received.[1]

---

1   Isaiah 53:3-5.

NOT WHY, BUT HOW

The Bible doesn't give us a complete answer on why suffering happens. But it does show us how to face it. The clearest example of this is the book of Job. God allowed him to lose his possessions, his health and his children. But he refused to curse God for this. "When God sends us something good, we welcome it. How can we complain when he sends us trouble?" *

* Job 2:10.

There's no escaping it. Religion **has** caused wars and division throughout history.

In the eleventh and twelfth centuries Christians fought 'Crusades' or holy wars to recapture the 'holy land' Palestine from Muslim invaders. In the thirteenth and fifteenth centuries the Church of Rome set up its 'Inquisition' to punish (by death, in extreme cases) any who disagreed with its teaching. In response, it became at times a capital offence to be a Roman Catholic in England and other Protestant countries; Roman Catholics only gradually gained equality under the law. And throughout 'Christian' Europe, Jews suffered the same sort of persecution.

As we know only too well, hatred and fighting in the name of religion continue to shock the world. Israelis and Arabs have lived in almost constant hostility since the modern state of Israel was founded in 1948, despite determined attempts at peace. The roots of their conflict go back to Old Testament times.

BLAME RELIGION

Many people react to this by deciding religion must be a bad thing. "Let's forget about religion," they say, "and just get on with loving other people."

It's a very understandable reaction. But I think it shows that the people who say it haven't thought much about it. And they certainly haven't tried it!

For one thing, loving other people is a lot harder than it sounds. Human beings naturally turn to hating and feuding when they feel under threat. It's only religion that has taught them that they **should** love their neighbours.

But they only turn to actual fighting when something **very important** is threatened. You can't imagine someone slugging their neighbour because they like a different brand of coffee or wear funny coloured shoes. Only if they have a row about something that really *matters* ...

That's why I actually expect religious wars. A religion isn't worth having unless it's the most important thing in life to me. And if it's the most important thing in my life, then I'm willing to fight for it, even die for it ... if someone else attacks it or tries to destroy it.

That's the way I naturally feel about my religion. And it's exactly the way many Muslims feel. Muslim leaders have declared a 'jihad' or holy war against Israel. And some have pronounced a 'fatwa' or death sentence on the author Salman Rushdie, because they believe his book *The Satanic Verses* insulted Islam.

But as a Christian, I find my religion telling me *not* to hurt or harm other people. So I must learn to control my aggressive instincts and love even those who attack my faith. This is more than I can do on my own. But Jesus loves his enemies, and his Spirit lives in me to teach me how.

Jesus' teaching in his Sermon on the Mount:

> Happy are those who work for peace; God will call them his children!
>
> ... love your enemies and pray for those who persecute you, so that you may become the children of your Father in heaven.[2]

CHRISTIANS AT WAR?
In Northern Ireland the two 'sides' who have been opposed to each other are frequently labelled Protestants and Catholics. This gives a horrific image to Christianity. It is quite true that there are Roman Catholic Christians and Protestant Christians living side by side in Northern Ireland. Their history means they have many differences between them. But within both communities, those with a living Christian faith are working hard for peace. We should join them in praying for the peace process to succeed.

By contrast, any who continue their threats to shoot and plant bombs do so for political rather than religious reasons and deny by their actions any Christian faith they ever had. It is far more accurate to label them extreme Unionists (or Loyalists) and Nationalists (or Republicans).

---

2 Matthew 5:9,44,45.

2.10 "Don't all religions worship the same God?"

Definitely a top ten entry in the turn of the century public opinion charts, this. And it was equally popular all through the 20th century. It influences RE in many schools. And it inspires the requests you sometimes hear for 'multi-faith services', bringing all religions together.

It's a nice friendly idea in a multi-racial world where people of different faiths live next door to each other. It's only polite to say, "Your religion is as good as mine. They're just different ways of worshipping the one real God."

But anyone who says this needs to think a little deeper. Hindus believe in many gods, not just one real one. And Buddhists don't believe in any god at all. So how can we all be talking about the same God? Many members of other faiths would be insulted and upset if we told them they believe the same as us.

It only confuses everything to pretend there are no differences. We can still be friendly and respect the good things about other religions, while looking at the important ways they differ from each other.

CHRISTIANITY AND ISLAM

Take two of the most common faiths in Britain.

They have the same background. Both take the Old Testament as one of their holy books. Both believe in one God. He's meant to be the same God. But is he really?

The Christian view of God is shaped by Jesus. Christians accept Jesus' claim that he's God in person and so shows us what God is like.

Muslims honour Jesus as a prophet. But they see God as far too holy to become a man on earth. They think Christians are blasphemous to worship Jesus as God.

Christians follow Jesus in believing the most important thing he came to do was to die for our sins on the cross. To them, this shows God at his most loving: at great cost to himself he finds a way to enable us to receive eternal life.

Muslims teach that God would never allow his prophet to suffer such a humiliating death. At the last moment before the crucifixion, God took Jesus to heaven. He swapped him for someone who looked like Jesus and died on the cross instead.

These are big differences. And they lead to a different understanding of what God is like.

Muslims *say* 'Allah' is loving and forgiving. But to Christian ears he sounds rather stern and frightening. This is partly because of holy wars and death threats to those who betray the faith. But also, I think, because of the way Muslims understand "God is one". They think of him as all on his own, distant and unapproachable. The very name 'Islam' means submission to his will.

Jesus, on the other hand, led Christians to see that God could also be one with a multiple oneness. He spoke of the Father and the Son and the Spirit all being one together.[1] They are a unity in the same sort of way a family is a unit.

He said these different 'members of the Godhead' or 'three persons in the one God' love each other and always have. And their love spills over to the creatures they have made.[2] The keynote of Christianity is love.[3]

So which is right?

To me, Jesus is the key.

Everything hinges on his claim to be God in person.[4] If he is *not*, the whole of Christianity collapses with him. Forget it, and try another religion.

But if he *is* God, then every other religion must be wrong at the points where it disagrees with him.

ARROGANT?

People call Christians arrogant for saying our faith is right and others are wrong. We certainly sound arrogant or smug sometimes; but there's no excuse for it. For we're not saying *we* have done anything good or clever. We're saying God has appeared and said, "Here I am. Follow me." In doing so, we're simply being obedient, not arrogant. Surely the real arrogance is to think you know better than him and tell him he's wrong.

Nor are we saying everything in other religions is wrong. They have many good and helpful things about them. Jewish family life, Muslim morality and Buddhist concern for the natural world have much to teach us. But, according to Jesus, they're not the way to find God. Indeed, in making it harder for their followers to think about Jesus with an open mind, they may be the opposite of what God wants.

But we don't say that to them when we first meet them. That *would* sound arrogant. We simply ask Jesus to help us befriend them and love them. The time to talk to them about him may come later.

Jesus claimed he was the founder of the only religion that can put people in touch with God.

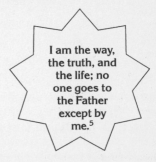

I am the way, the truth, and the life; no one goes to the Father except by me.[5]

Peter echoed the claim when he began to preach the Good News.

Salvation is to be found through him [Jesus] alone; in all the world there is no one else whom God has given who can save us.[6]

---

1 See 2.11 "How can God be one and three at the same time?" (page 54).

2 John 17:24,26.

3 As in Jesus' summary of God's law: love God and love your neighbour (Mark 12:29-31).

4 See 3.3 "Jesus was just a good man" (page 64).

5 John 14:6.

6 Acts 4:12.

2.11 "How can God be one and three at the same time?"

They weren't being deliberately awkward, you know. Those early Christians with that stuff about 'God in three persons — blessed Trinity!'

They didn't dream it all up as brain-torture. They were forced into the idea by the events in front of their eyes.

GOD IS ONE

Most of them had been fed the Old Testament with their mother's milk. They could recite its traditional creed with complete certainty: "The LORD our God, the LORD is *one*."[1] Every fibre of logic in them proved that therefore a man couldn't be God as well.

But Jesus stood before them and calmly unstitched their logic. Although completely a man, down to his finger-prints and toenails, his every speech and action announced: "I'm God".[2] And if that sounded fantastic, any other explanation of him was even more screwy.

"What's more," he said, "when I go, my life will continue through my Spirit who is also God like me, yet different."[3]

That's exactly what they found. It was as if Jesus was still with them; still talking to them, leading, helping. Yet now he was invisible, somehow *inside* them.

But surely, wasn't Jesus back in heaven, his Father's right-hand man? They'd seen him go themselves.[4]

GOD IS THREE

Their brains hurt! God was cracking their minds open to replace the old belief with a new one that better fitted the facts. One God — OK. But a God apparently with *three* names.

Sometimes there was overlap, but sometimes they had clearly different functions. It didn't seem to matter whether you spoke of the *Spirit* living in you, or of

Jesus and the *Father*.[5] Nor whether you prayed to "Our Father" or "Lord Jesus".[6]

On the other hand, God the Father hadn't left heaven while Jesus was on earth. And it did help to see all three of God's 'faces' involved in helping us to know him and pray to him: "*through Christ* ... all of us ... are able to come *in the one Spirit* into the presence of *the Father*"[7].

GOD IS THREE-IN-ONE

Previously they'd thought — as a Muslim still does — in terms of *mathematical* unity: 'one is one and all alone, and evermore shall be so!' Now they learnt God's oneness was an *organic* unity. All sorts of organisms are three-and-yet-one. Mum, Dad and baby make up one family. 'Trinity oaks' look at a distance like three trees, but really all stem from one trunk. Clover leaves are three-in-one. Musical triads are three notes, but one harmonious chord. The substance known as H_2O can appear as water, ice or steam.

So we needn't be surprised at a similar three-in-oneness in God. He'd hinted at it from the very first words in the Bible. "In the beginning ... God created the universe". The Hebrew for 'God' is a plural noun; but the verb 'created' is singular. "Then God said, 'And now *we* will make human beings; they will be like *us* and resemble *us*.'"[8]

The Old Testament doesn't show God as a 'mathematical' One. From the start there's a 'we' and an 'us' about him. Jesus and the New Testament bring the picture into sharp focus: 'We' are the rich oneness of Father, Son and Holy Spirit.

We get direct benefits from this richness. We belong to God three times over, as a house 'belongs' to builder, owner, and occupier. The Father designed us; Jesus bought us by dying for us on the cross; the Spirit says, "You are my home".

These two pages of plodding words can't capture the whole truth about the living God! The 'Trinity' (three-in-one) is the best description of God we have; yet we're still left guessing. God has shown us a lot about himself, but he stays a mystery. Although we catch glimpses of him, he's far, far too big for us to hold in one snapshot.

Thank God he is! A God we could parcel up into a neat 20-minute sermon or a paperback book like this would be a God not worth knowing. But the God who is Almighty Father, Jesus Christ, Holy Spirit, rolled into one for ever and ever meets every need of human nature.

Jesus taught his followers to proclaim the one-in-three God at the heart of their message:

> Go, then, to all peoples everywhere and make them my disciples: baptize them in the name of the Father, the Son, and the Holy Spirit, and teach them to obey everything I have commanded you.[9]

Paul was the first to think up the Trinity blessing which commits everything we know about each other to everything we know about God.

The grace of the Lord Jesus Christ, the love of God, and the fellowship of the Holy Spirit be with you all.[10]

---

1 Deuteronomy 6:4 New International Version.
2 For examples, see 3.3 "Jesus was just a good man" (page 64).
3 John 14:16-18.
4 Acts 1:9; and Stephen — Acts 7:55-56.
5 John 14:17,23.
6 Matthew 6:9; Acts 7:59.
7 Ephesians 2:18.
8 Genesis 1:26.
9 Matthew 28:19,20.
10 2 Corinthians 13:13 (Good News Bible; verse 14 in New International Version).

THE NICENE CREED

A statement of faith which aimed to counter false teaching that presented Jesus as less than fully God. It was drawn up by a council of bishops meeting at Nicaea in AD 325.

**We believe in one God,
the Father, the almighty,
maker of heaven and earth...**

**We believe in one Lord, Jesus Christ,
the only Son of God,
eternally begotten of the Father,
God from God, Light from Light,
true God from true God,
begotten, not made,
of one Being with the Father...**

**We believe in the Holy Spirit,
the Lord, the giver of life,
who proceeds from the Father and the Son.
With the Father and the Son he is worshipped and glorified ...**

THE TRINITY

The word 'Trinity' never appears in the Bible. But it expresses what the Bible teaches, and what the first Christians had come to believe. The Father and Jesus and the Holy Spirit are all God.

This is a vital difference between Bible-believing Christians and some other groups who sometimes claim to be Christians (e.g. Jehovah's Witnesses). They do not believe in the Trinity, because they do not believe Jesus and the Spirit are God.*

* For more on these sub-Christian groups, go to 6.9 "What is heresy?" (page 161).

2.12 "What does God do all the time?"

'A day in the life of God' sounds very different from your or my average day. He has no getting up or going to bed time — because he never goes to bed, and never sleeps!

He's awake round-the-clock to hear and answer people's prayers. This activity alone has no slack time in it, because while the Christians in Britain are asleep, those in Australia are up and praying, and so on ...

But beyond that, he's not only dealing with us Christians. We're the people who've already said yes to the special relationship he offers everyone. But he loves the whole world and he's busy at work in it.

He didn't just create the universe and then sit back in an armchair to watch it spinning in space. He keeps the whole thing going. If he stopped holding it together, it would all fall apart.[1]

His burning passion in the world is for justice and peace and love. He cares about the needs and rights of the downtrodden and oppressed. Where they are honoured and helped, he's pleased. Where they are cheated and forgotten, he's angry and plans to step in. Sooner or later, in this life or the next, he will act on their behalf.

He's working on a vast building project, and everything is part of that. Sometimes the New Testament refers to it as a building or temple for God to live in; but the 'building blocks' are human lives willingly handed over to God to fit into his grand design.[2]

Jesus called the project God's kingdom, and it was the commonest theme of his teaching.[3] He didn't mean a country on the map, as God's Old Testament people had been. He meant the lives of people who serve God as their king, and put his will and values into action. The project has been under way for 2000 years already, but will only be complete at the end of time.

Meanwhile, at any given moment, God's fingers are at work in millions of encounters and relationships all round the world. Unlike us, he's not limited to thinking and doing one thing at a time. He is boundless, endless energy.

The protector of Israel never dozes or sleeps.
The LORD will guard you; he is by your side to protect you.[4]

All of them [the things you have made] depend on you to give them food when they need it.
You give it to them, and they eat it; you provide food, and they are satisfied.
When you turn away, they are afraid; when you take away your breath, they die and go back to the dust from which they came.
But when you give them breath, they are created; you give new life to the earth.[5]

Paul tells Gentile Christians they are as much part of God's building project as Jewish Christians.

> You, too, are built upon the foundation laid by the apostles and prophets, the cornerstone being Christ Jesus himself. He is the one who holds the whole building together and makes it grow into a sacred temple dedicated to the Lord. In union with him you too are being built together with all the others into a place where God lives through his Spirit.[6]

1. How would you answer someone who says it's impossible to believe in God in our world of modern science and technology?
2. What evidence have you got personally that God really exists? Which parts of it do you find most convincing?
3. What one truth about God would you most want to get across to (a) someone who says they have lost their faith through the way they have suffered; (b) a Christian trying to help someone who is suffering? How would you set about expressing that truth to them?
4. How would you answer a Christian who says they don't understand the Trinity, and it's not important anyway?
5. How would you defend the Christian idea of God to (a) a New Ager who says it's much too narrow; and (b) a militant feminist who says it's much too male?
6. Analyse a typical day. How far do you depend on God, and how far on other things? Are you happy with this balance, or would you like to change it in any way?

---

1 Psalm 104:27,30. Compare Hebrews 1:3; Colossians 1:17.

2 1 Peter 2:5.

3 E.g. Mark 4:30-32. For more about the kingdom of God, go to 6.6 "What's the connection between the Church and other Christian groups?" (page 155).

4 Psalm 121:4,5.

5 Psalm 104:27-30.

6 Ephesians 2:20-22.

How can someone who lived 2000 years ago have anything to say to us today?

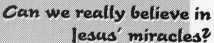
How could Jesus be born of a virgin mother?

Can we really believe in Jesus' miracles?

3

GOD'S SON

Jesus

3

GOD'S SON

3.1 "How can someone who lived 2000 years ago have anything to say to us today?"

In a world where computers go out-of-date every few months, 2000 years ago seems unbelievably primitive.

Yet Jesus of Nazareth remains big news and box office. Every two or three years another book or film about him tops the charts. Meanwhile the original 'book of the film' (the Bible) is the best seller ever.

The media sometimes try to show Jesus' followers as a dying breed. They simply don't know what's going on. In Africa south of the Sahara desert, in South America and in East Asia the Christian churches are growing faster than the population rate. That means the proportion of Christians in those countries is going up and up. If it doesn't stop, it'll reach 100%!

Even in the cynical, materialistic West there are far more Christians than you would imagine from watching TV or reading the newspapers. There are many more people in church services on Sunday mornings than at football matches on Saturday afternoons.

What's more, they're not just people who were brought up that way. Many of them were not born or brought up as Christians at all. Some are famous, most are ordinary; some old, many young. What links them is that they have changed from a quite different background to follow Jesus.

Why?

THE MOST IMPORTANT PERSON IN HISTORY

Jesus isn't just someone who lived in the first century and happened to get into the history books. He's the centre point of world history. Everyone else dates their birthday by the calendar; but Jesus dates the calendar by his birthday. He's the person BC and AD refer to!

Jesus said he was more than an ordinary human being. He claimed to be God himself, come to earth as a man.[1] He chose that moment to make himself known. But as God he belongs to all centuries and generations.

That would explain why his teaching is still right up-to-date. "Your heart will always be where your riches are." "Can any of you live a bit longer by worrying about it?" "There is more happiness in giving than in receiving."[2] This is not about the latest technology or the news of the day. It's about human nature. So it never goes out of date.

The way he lived is just as instructive as his teaching. One of his closest friends summed up his life as "he went everywhere, doing good".[3] We need that sort of person today — perhaps more than ever before — in our world of rising crime and people in need.

Most important of all, Jesus' biggest achievement is still a matter of life and death to every single human being.

> There was no other good enough
> to pay the price of sin;
> He, only, could unlock the gate
> of heaven — and let us in.[4]

If you want to go to heaven, you need Jesus. Your wrongdoing disqualifies you from entering God's presence. But as he died, Jesus took the penalty for all the wrongs we'd ever done. He made it possible for us to be forgiven.[5]

STILL ALIVE NOW

When he died, he didn't stay dead.[6] He came back to life and returned to heaven.[7] He's alive there now to hear and help anyone who needs him. Everyone who has asked him has found him ready to help at once. That includes yesterday and this morning as well as way back in history.

Quite simply, he is God's good news for the whole human race. Not only in his own generation, but in every generation before it and after it. That makes him vitally important to every person in every age —the 21st century as much as the first.

He has everything to say to people today. We shall miss the whole point of life if we ignore him.

Jesus said:

> I have come in order that you might have life — life in all its fullness.[8]

One of the first church leaders said:

> Jesus Christ is the same yesterday, today, and for ever.[9]
>
> Jesus lives on for ever ... And so he is able, now and always, to save those who come to God through him, because he lives for ever to plead with God for them.[10]

---

1 John 8:23,24, where Jesus claims God's name (Exodus 3:13-15) for himself. See also 3.4 "How could Jesus be born of a virgin mother?" (page 66).

2 Matthew 6:21,27; Acts 20:35.

3 Acts 10:38.

4 From 'There is a green hill far away' by Mrs Cecil F. Alexander (1818-95).

5 Ephesians 1:7. See also 3.9 "Why did God need to send his Son to die for us?" (page 77).

6 See 3.7 "How can we believe Jesus came back to life from the dead?" (page 72).

7 See 3.11 "Where is Jesus now?" (page 80).

8 John 10:10.

9 Hebrews 13:8.

10 Hebrews 7:24,25.

3.2 "Are the records of Jesus' life really true?"

This is a very important question. Christianity rests totally on what Jesus is reported to have said and done. If we can't rely on the 'Gospels' — the four books in the Bible which record his life (Matthew, Mark, Luke and John) — we shall never know whether or not Christianity is true.

There are several different things about Jesus' life which people today find hard to believe. That he was actually God. That his mother was a virgin. That he never did anything wrong. That he performed miracles. That he came back to life after he died. The next few pages take each of these amazing ideas in turn.

Here we simply ask, "Can we trust the Gospels in general?"

People are often suspicious of writers who are biased. Obviously the Gospel writers were Christians. So mightn't they have made the whole thing up? Or at least made Jesus out to be much more perfect and powerful than he really was?

UNBIASED SUPPORT

Non-Christian historians from about the same time support what the Gospel writers say. Not in detail, of course. From their point of view, Jesus was just a small-town carpenter turned wandering Jewish teacher. He didn't seem that important.

But a variety of Jewish, Roman and other pagan writers make clear they know Jesus was

(a) born in an unusual way;

(b) known as a miracle worker who claimed to be God;

(c) killed on a cross in mysteriously darkened daylight;

(d) said to have been seen alive again by his followers, who expected him to come back from heaven to earth in the future;

(e) worshipped as God by Christians.[1]

RELIABLE SOURCES

We don't have to write off the Gospel writers as hopelessly biased. They were trustworthy historians. Many people in the ancient world might have made up fabulous legends about their gods. But three of the four writers were Jews. They were brought up from birth to tell the truth and treat religious teaching with the deepest reverence. They would expect God to punish them severely if they spread false ideas about him. The fourth writer, Luke, was not a Jew, but stresses in his book how careful he has been to check that everything he reports is true.[2]

Even when they — like Luke — didn't see or hear the events they describe, they're reporting the memories of those who *were* there. Mark's Gospel is almost certainly the story as told by Peter. And although it may not have been written down till 30 years later, Peter was preaching the story by word of mouth from the first few weeks after Jesus died.[3]

If he and the others felt free to 'improve' the story in the telling, you would expect their own performance to appear in a good light. But Peter is almost always shown making mistakes. He's hardly likely to have made them up![4]

We can even take the reported words of Jesus as much more accurate than we would expect. There were no cassette-players then, and very few books. So Jewish teachers put their words into poetic rhythm which their followers would find it easy to learn by heart. Much of Jesus' recorded teaching is of this kind. And — sure enough — when some scholars translated it back into Aramaic, the language Jesus actually spoke — it turned into poetry.[5]

It's up to people who want *not* to believe the Gospels to try to prove them wrong.

Luke seems to have written his Gospel for someone called Theophilus — perhaps an important official who became a Christian.[6] This is how he starts the book:

> **Dear Theophilus:**
> Many people have done their best to write a report of the things that have taken place among us. They wrote what we have been told by those who saw these things from the beginning and who proclaimed the message. And so, your Excellency, because I have carefully studied all these matters from their beginning, I thought it would be good to write an orderly account for you. I do this so that you will know the full truth about everything which you have been taught.[7]

JESUS: THE EVIDENCE

Josephus published his *Antiquities of the Jews* in AD 93 to give the Jews a better image with the Romans. He wasn't a Christian, but this is what he wrote about Jesus in the section on Pontius Pilate's time as governor.

> And there arose about this time Jesus, a wise man, if indeed we should call him a man; for he was a doer of marvellous deeds, a teacher of men who receive the truth with pleasure. He won over many Jews and also many Greeks. This man was the Messiah. And when Pilate had condemned him to the cross at the instigation of our own leaders, those who had loved him from the first did not cease. For he appeared to them on the third day alive again, as the holy prophets had predicted and said many other wonderful things about him. And even now the race of Christians, so named after him, has not yet died out.*

---

1 No room here to list all these writers, but you can find out in Michael Green's book, **World on the Run** (IVP, 1983) pp. 27-36.

2 See Luke 1:1-4, quoted above.

3 We also possess far more copies and far older copies of the Gospels than of any other surviving books from the first century. See 5.9 "Hasn't the Bible been changed over the years?" (page 132).

4 This is in complete contrast to Jesus, who never appears to put a foot wrong. The Gospels are the only life-stories ever written where the central character is never criticised. See 3.5 "How could Jesus be perfect?" (page 68).

5 In addition, Jesus promised the Holy Spirit would bring all he had said back to the apostles' memories (John 14:26). See 5.2 "How can the Bible actually help us?" (page 116).

6 Or "Theophilus" could be a code-name for any Christian reader. It simply means 'God-lover'.

7 Luke 1:1-4.

---

* *Antiquities of the Jews* 18.3.3.

63

3
GOD'S SON

3.3 "Jesus was just a good man and great teacher like other great teachers."

He *wasn't* like other teachers, you know. The people who heard him thought he was quite different.[1] At various times he left them amazed, impressed, shocked, silenced, put off, angry, even goaded to murder him.[2]

If that surprises us, it's because we've grown immune to his words. He made mind-blowing claims about himself, quite unlike what anyone else has ever said. They're in poetic picture language, and so they don't have the shocking impact on us that they did for his first hearers. We need to unwrap them to get at what he's saying.

THE GREAT I AM

"I am the bread of life. Those who come to me will never be hungry; those who believe in me will never be thirsty."[3] In other words, if we're to be spiritually alive at all, we need Jesus as desperately as we need food and drink to stay physically alive. And if we have him (i.e. if we're Christians), he will satisfy us fully.

"I am the light of the world. Whoever follows me will have the light of life and will never walk in darkness."[4] He leads us to the meaning of life. But without him we're lost.

"I am the gate. Whoever comes in by me will be saved ... I am the good shepherd, who is willing to die for the sheep."[5] The Palestinian shepherd lay across the doorway of the sheepfold at night as the line of resistance between the sheep and the wolves. Jesus protects us from harm in this life and hell in the next.

"I am the resurrection and the life. Those who believe in me will live, even though they die; and all those who live and believe in me will never die."[6] Jesus

is the key to eternal life in heaven after we die.

"I am the way, the truth, and the life; no one goes to the Father except by me."[7] Jesus is the only way to find God and meet him.

"I am the vine, and you are the branches ... you can do nothing without me."[8] Vine and branches were an Old Testament picture of God's people on earth. Without Jesus we can't belong to God and become the people we have it in us to be.

To his first hearers the most shocking words of all these were the constantly repeated "I am". All Jews know them as God's personal name.[9] When Jesus took them on his own lips, people understood clearly he was saying he was God. They tried to execute him for blasphemy.[10]

On their terms, they were quite right. Anyone who says things like this is *not* just a good man and great teacher. He's either much more or much less. If he's wrong, he must be sick or evil. If he's right, he's nothing short of God himself.

Which is what he said he was.

GOD IN PERSON

Christians follow Jesus in believing he was God as well as a man.[11]

This makes him a one-off. Buddha and Muhammad, for example, were great teachers and, by the standards of their day, good men. But they never for one moment thought or said they were God. And no-one else thought it either.[12]

There's a popular idea today that all religious leaders are equally 'sons of God' and 'full of the Christ Spirit'. But it doesn't stand up for a moment beside the towering difference between Jesus and all others. The only way you can say Jesus *is* a good man and great teacher is to agree with him that he's **also** God's one and only Son.

> ... the High Priest questioned him, "Are you the Messiah, the Son of the Blessed God?"
>
> "I am," answered Jesus ...[13]

1   Mark 1:22.
2   E.g. Luke 4:32,15; Mark 10:24; 12:34; John 6:60,61; Luke 4:28; John 8:37.
3   John 6:35.
4   John 8:12.
5   John 10:9,11.
6   John 11:25,26.
7   John 14:6.
8   John 15:5.
9   Exodus 3:14.
10 John 8:24,58,59.
11 3.4 "How could Jesus be born of a virgin mother?" (page 66) explores this further.
12 This is a crucial difference between Christianity and other faiths. See 2.10 "Don't all religions worship the same God?" (page 52). Some people do worship Buddha today; but this idea crept into Buddhism centuries after Buddha himself.
13 Mark 14:61,62.

3.4 "How could Jesus be born of a virgin mother?"

Some species reproduce themselves by 'parthenogenesis' or virgin birth. That means an egg or new shoot develops without any help from a male. Species like dandelions, some insects, and some fish.

But not, as a rule, human beings.

Human reproduction normally needs a male to have sex with a female and fertilise the 'ovum' or egg inside her.[1] And once a girl has had sex with a man — even just once — she's not a virgin any more.

So either Mary wasn't a virgin when she conceived Jesus, or something very unusual was going on.

That's what the Bible claims — something very unusual. God caused her to become pregnant without having sex.

If God is really God, there's no reason why he shouldn't. He could override the usual mechanism any time he likes. He could cause any number of people to be born of virgin mothers.

But he says he has chosen to do it only once — for his own Son — when the time came for him to be born on earth as a human being.

GOD BECOMING A MAN

We can't begin to understand *how* Jesus was conceived in this way. But the more important question is *why* was he?

The answer is, he was a uniquely unusual baby. Unlike us, he did not start life at conception. He was already alive before that. He had been for ever.[2] He is God the Son, every bit as eternal as God the Father.

But now he was to become a human being. The plan was for him to make God known to us; to show us what he's like in the language we can best understand — a human life.[3] So while he was a 100% real human being in every breath and brain cell, he was also 100% real God.

This means there's a quick but completely satisfying answer to the question, 'What is God like?' The answer is, 'God is like Jesus. Find out about him.'[4] It also means God has an equally satisfying answer to the question, 'What is human life like?' He knows, because he's been through it in Jesus. He fully understands all the trials and temptations we face.[5]

Stage 2 of the plan was for him to deal with the human problem. We have all rebelled against God. None of us is good enough to put matters right with God for *ourselves*, let alone for the whole human race. It needed someone who was both human and divine to bring us back together again.[6]

How could this God-man come to be? No mere man could make himself God. But God is quite able to be born as a human baby and live a human life. In Jesus he did. 'Conceived by the Holy Spirit' —Son of God. 'Born of the virgin Mary' —son of a human mother.

> God sent the angel Gabriel to ... Mary ... The angel said to her, "... You will become pregnant and give birth to a son ... He will ... be called the Son of the Most High God." Mary said to the angel, "I am a virgin. How, then, can this be?" The angel answered, "The Holy Spirit will come on you, and God's power will rest upon you ... For there is nothing that God cannot do."[7]

A BELIEF TOO FAR?

You may have friends who say I can't become a Christian if I have to believe in the Virgin Birth. Many people seem to find this a stumbling-block. But this is getting things in the wrong order. They don't have to believe everything in the Bible before they can be Christians. But once they *do* become Christians, they'll find the Virgin Birth makes more sense.

So tell them to lay it on one side for the moment. The important thing is to start following the Jesus who was God-and-man, not to understand the mechanics of how he came to be both at once.

At the same time, two of the Gospels — Matthew and Luke — state explicitly that the mechanism was virgin birth. And John's Gospel implies it repeatedly by describing Jesus as coming "from above" and "from heaven".* Mary's reaction to all this was, "I am the Lord's servant ... May it happen ... as you have said."** It is a good example of humble acceptance for us to follow.

1   Modern genetic science has introduced variations on this. But there were none, of course, at the time of Jesus' birth.
2   Colossians 1:15-17; John 1:1,2.
3   Hebrews 1:2,3.
4   John 1:18; 14:8,9. See 2.5 "What's God like?" (page 42).
5   Hebrews 4:15.
6   1 Timothy 2:5,6.
7   Luke 1:26-37.

* E.g. John 3:31.
** Luke 1:38.

3.5 "How could Jesus be perfect if he was human?"

The Bible is never hypocritical. It doesn't pretend its heroes are perfect when they aren't. Abraham, Moses, David, Peter — all appear with their glaring faults unmasked.[1]

But it constantly claims Jesus never did anything wrong. Friends, enemies and neutral observers all agreed they could find no fault in him.[2] On one occasion he even challenged his critics, "Which one of you can prove that I am guilty of sin?"[3] As far as we can tell from the record, no-one even replied. But Jesus went still further. He didn't just say he never sinned; he put it the positive way round and said, "I always do what pleases God".[4]

We find this almost impossible to understand. We are flawed through and through, so we can't imagine somebody perfect. When Jesus was a child, for instance, did he *never* get into trouble?[5]

But if Jesus really was God living a human life, it's only reasonable to expect him to make no mistakes. There's nothing surprising in the Bible claiming he never did anything wrong. He was the God-man showing how people ought to live.

TEMPER, TEMPER?

The trouble is, some people think he did behave badly — at least on one or two occasions. Usually they're thinking about his anger.

One time was when he drove animals and money-changers out of the Temple with a whip. He said, "God said, 'My Temple will be called a house of prayer for the people of all nations'. But you have turned it into a hideout for thieves!"[6] Imagine what the tabloids today would make of a crusading vicar rampaging down the aisles in Tescos because it opened out of hours on a Sunday!

The interesting thing is, Jesus' followers said that as they watched him they were reminded of another bit of the Bible. It says, "My devotion to your house, O God, burns in me like a fire."[7]

In other words, they didn't pretend Jesus wasn't angry — they said it was sinless anger. There is such a thing as 'righteous indignation' — even if *we* never quite achieve it. Our anger always trips over the edge into sin, usually because it's for a selfish reason. But Jesus was angry for a **selfless** reason — because he couldn't bear to see the building meant to be a meeting-point with God hijacked as a money-grabbing market place.

The Gospels show Jesus getting angry several times. But it's always anger at people being hurt or God's creation being spoiled.[8] It's good, clean, perfect anger.

But because we're imperfect people, and our experience of anger is warped, we tend to feel uncomfortable about two of these other incidents when Jesus seemed to react angrily. Both involve the natural world.

FIGS AND PIGS

One occasion was when he put a curse on a fig tree, and the next day its leaves withered. The other was when he sent evil spirits out of an oppressed man into a herd of pigs which stampeded into the sea and were drowned.[9]

But to Jesus people matter more than plants or animals. The fig tree was a well known symbol or illustration of God's people. He used it to warn of God's coming judgment on those who were not producing the 'fruit' of obeying him.

The pigs showed everyone present — including the poor, terrorised man — that the evil spirits had well and truly come out of him. In God's eyes the well-being of one person is worth any number of pigs.[10]

If you're worried about the farmer who owned the pigs ... he must have felt as sick as any farmer today losing livestock to disease or a flood. A disaster, but not the end of the world.

In fact for this man, it could have been a whole new start to *his* world. It was a chance to meet Jesus and learn to value things his way.

The perfect human being who's also God is not always a cosy or predictable person to be with. But how can we ever do things right ourselves without him?

Peter and John, two of Jesus' closest friends, both said he never did anything wrong:

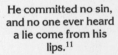

> He committed no sin, and no one ever heard a lie come from his lips.[11]
>
> You know that Christ appeared in order to take away sins, and that there is no sin in him.[12]

3 God's Son

1   This is especially important in the case of Peter. See 3.2 "Are the records of Jesus' life really true?" (page 62).

2   For the friends, see Peter and John's comments above. For an example of Jesus' enemies, see Pilate's verdict in Luke 23:4. For a neutral onlooker, take the criminal on the cross beside him (Luke 23:41).

3   John 8:46.

4   John 8:29.

5   We only know of one incident from his childhood, his family's annual Passover visit to Jerusalem when he was 12 (Luke 2:41-51). He stayed in the temple after the rest of the pilgrims set off for home. His mother was frightened at losing him and in effect told him off. His disarming reply shows he was not aware of doing anything wrong: "Didn't you know that I had to be in my Father's house?" Luke describes the rest of his childhood as the model, perfect adolescence. "Jesus grew both in body and in wisdom, gaining favour with God and men" (2:52).

6   Mark 11:17.

7   John 2:17 quoting Psalm 69:9.

8   Other examples are Mark 3:5 and 10:14.

9   Mark 11:12-14,20,21; 5:1-20.

10 Besides, we haven't got God's complete view of what happens when he exorcises evil spirits. For all we know, there was no other way in this case to stop them continuing their demonic activity — if not in this man, then in someone else.

11 1 Peter 2:22.

12 1 John 3:5.

3.6 "Can we really believe in Jesus' miracles?"

The 21st century West is not comfortable with the idea of miracles. They appear to be abnormal events which you can't explain. We like to think we're in control, with a scientific explanation for everything that happens.

So people have dreamed up some weird explanations of what Jesus must *really* have done. He was so plausible a 'faith-healer' that when he said people would get better, they trusted him and began to *feel* better at once. He didn't *really* feed 5000 people on next to nothing; but his teaching persuaded first one boy, then everyone else, to share their packed lunches together.

I can't help feeling that if you believe that really explains the stories in the Gospels, you're a lot more gullible than anyone who takes them at face value.

The Gospels are full of stories of Jesus performing miracles. I once got hold of a small, giveaway copy of Mark's Gospel. I cut out all the stories of miracles to see how much was left. It was just a few wispy shreds of paper.

SON OF GOD

If Jesus was just any old person like you or me, of course we'd be right to smell a rat in all these stories. But he said he was more than any old person — God's Son, no less.[1]

If he's right — if he *is* God in person — what's so strange about him being able to control the 'laws' of nature? He invented them, after all.

In any case, these so-called 'laws' are not binding. They are simply our observation of how things usually happen. In normal circumstances, people can't walk on water or bring the dead back to life. But Jesus is God as well as a human being. He brings a whole new set of powers into play. If you or I could walk across Lake Galilee or command Lazarus to come out of his grave, it would indeed be a miracle. But with Jesus, 'it stands to reason' because of who he is. For him it's natural, not really miraculous at all. It would be more suspicious if he *didn't* perform any 'miracles'.

They seem like miracles to us, but aren't they just the sort of thing you'd expect God to do? None of them was out of character or harmful. He didn't strike people blind; he made them see. He didn't make people drop dead; he brought them back to life.

What's more, he didn't do them to get any reward for himself. He charged no fee and tried to avoid publicity.[2] He performed 'miracles' because he cared about people suffering.[3] And he gave all the credit to his Father, who gave him the power to do them.[4]

SIGNS OF GOD

Jesus' miracles weren't just flashy conjuring tricks to brighten up a dull evening. They were, as he himself called them, 'signs'.[5] They show us something deep and permanent about God.

That's good news. If the only thing we can learn from Jesus' miracles is that he was God on earth, they haven't got much interest for us today. But if they also show something that he wants to do for *us*, they're as full of meaning now as they were in the first place.

We can't walk on water or tell a storm to shut up, but Jesus could. That shows God controls the forces of nature. We can never be beyond the reach of his protection.

Jesus fed the hungry and even laid on extra wine at a wedding. That shows God can provide our needs. And more than that, he wants us to enjoy life at a deeper level than our needs alone.

He cured people and raised them from death. That shows God won't let illness and death have the last word. When we start following Jesus we receive everlasting life; although our bodies die, we're totally sure of going to heaven to continue our lives in the next and better instalment. There we shall enjoy perfect health. In this life God gives us no magic protection from illness, though he often does cure us — usually through natural processes, but sometimes supernaturally.[6]

I not only believe Jesus' miracles. I find them exciting, because they tell me so much about God.

Peter witnessed most of Jesus' miracles. He was in no doubt what they showed about Jesus.

Jesus of Nazareth was a man whose divine authority was clearly proven to you by all the miracles and wonders which God performed through him ... All the people of Israel, then, are to know for sure that this Jesus, whom you crucified, is the one that God has made Lord and Messiah![202]

---

1   See 3.3 "Jesus was just a good man" (page 64).
2   E.g. Mark 1:43-45.
3   E.g. John 11:32-39.
4   E.g. John 11:40-42.
5   This is the literal meaning of the word Good News Bible translates as 'miracles' in, for example, John 6:26.

6   For more on heaven, go to 7.3 "What will heaven be like?" (page 170). For more on miraculous healing, go to 4.10 "Why doesn't the Holy Spirit heal everyone who's ill?" (page 106).
7   Acts 2:22,36.

3.7 "How can we believe Jesus came back to life from the dead?"

Many people think this is just a made-up happy ending tacked on to a sad story. It certainly *is* a happy ending. Jesus' friends were crumpled to think they wouldn't see him again. So they were over the moon when he came back into the room even more alive than before.[1]

But I don't think it's made up. And it's very important for Christians that it shouldn't be. We've put our trust in Jesus' promise to give us eternal life, and take us to heaven when we die.[2] That's not much good to us if he's still dead himself.

So how can we be sure 2000 years later that he really did come back to life?[3]

FACT 1 — JESUS' BODY DEFINITELY DISAPPEARED FROM THE GRAVE

The Christians were preaching in public that he was alive again a mere seven weeks after the event. And only a few hundred metres from where it happened! They couldn't have done it if the Roman authorities still had the body to prove them wrong.

Indeed, the authorities put out a story that the Christians had stolen the body.[4] But if they knew they were telling a lie, would they all have carried on saying he was alive? Would they have gone all the way to being martyred for saying it? And how could they teach that telling the truth was a basic part of their lifestyle?

FACT 2 — JESUS DEFINITELY APPEARED AFTER DEATH TO HIS FOLLOWERS

This is the evidence the New Testament majors on. It records appearances to Mary Magdalene and other women with her[5]; to the eleven apostles and to two other disciples on their way home from the city.[6]

Paul lists still other appearances — to James and himself.[7]

There was even a group of 500 of them prepared to swear they all saw him at the same time.[8] This couldn't just be wish-fulfilment, because hallucinations and ghosts don't appear to a whole crowd at once. Only a few extra-sensitive people see them.

In any case, they were not hyping themselves up into a hysterical state of longing and wishing to see him alive again. Their grief had blotted his promise to bounce back to life out of their minds. When the apostles first heard reports that he'd been seen, they thought it was emotional women dreaming it up.[9] They knew as well as we do that dead men don't come back. It took the real Jesus really there to convince them.[10]

FACT 3 — SINCE THEN MILLIONS OF CHRISTIANS WORLDWIDE HAVE CLAIMED JESUS IS MORE THAN JUST A MEMORY OR A DREAM

They're aware of him in their lives as a living presence.

This is hard to explain to someone who hasn't yet become a Christian. But it's incredible how Christians who've never met before, find they've had the same experience and understand each other completely. How could it happen if Jesus isn't alive and active through his invisible Spirit?

This combination of facts — the events at the time of Jesus' death and the experience of Christians ever since — led Dr Thomas Arnold, one of the most influential educationists in 19th century England, to make an extremely bold claim. He said the resurrection of Jesus was the best attested fact in history — i.e. the event with the most evidence that it really did happen.

That's worth thinking about.

Jesus repeatedly taught in advance that he would return to life after he died.

> Then Jesus began to teach his disciples: "The Son of Man[11] must suffer much and be rejected by the elders, the chief priests, and the teachers of the Law. He will be put to death, but three days later he will rise to life." He made this very clear to them.[12]

Paul was totally convinced Jesus was alive, because he had seen him. And he understood the vital importance of this truth to the Christian faith.

> If Christ has not been raised from death, then we have nothing to preach and you have nothing to believe.[13]

1 John 20:19,20.
2 E.g. John 10:28; 14:1-3.
3 Some people have suggested Jesus didn't really die on the cross. So, they say, he didn't reappear alive from the dead; he was still alive the first time round! But the executioners knew what they were doing. They certified him dead. And an eyewitness noticed something which only became recognised as clear evidence of death in the 20th century. Jesus' blood had separated into a dark red clot and watery serum (John 19:33-35).
4 Matthew 28:11-15.
5 Matthew 28:9,10.
6 Luke 24:13-35.
7 1 Corinthians 15:7,8.
8 1 Corinthians 15:6.
9 Luke 24:8-11.
10 The case of Thomas is the classic example of this (John 20:24-29).
11 Jesus often used the title "Son of Man" to describe himself. See 3.8 "What do people mean when they call Jesus the Messiah?" (page 74).
12 Mark 8:31,32; see also 9:31, 10:34.
13 1 Corinthians 15:14.

3

GOD'S
SON

3.8 "What do people mean when they call Jesus the Messiah?"

When your country has suffered disappointment or defeat, people want to be cheered up. They look round for new heroes — usually political leaders or sporting champions. When they find a potential world-beater, she or he becomes an almost religious figure. People talk of the new 'saviour'. Or even, borrowing the Bible word, a new 'Messiah'.

This was the atmosphere Jesus grew up in. His country had a proud history. His people were specially chosen by God. But now they were totally powerless, two small provinces of the Roman empire — Judea and Galilee.

KING

People looked wistfully into the Old Testament and found promises that one day the kingdom of Israel would be restored. There would once again be a great king like David.

Isaiah foretold his birth like this.

A child is born to us!
A son is given to us!
And he will be our ruler ...

His royal power will continue to grow;
his kingdom will always be at peace.
He will rule as King David's successor,
basing his power on right and justice,
from now until the end of time.[1]

There can be no doubt Jesus fulfilled this prophecy. Especially when we remember the amazing words in the middle of it.

He will be called,
"Wonderful Counsellor",
"Mighty God", "Eternal Father",
"Prince of Peace".

But the general idea in Jesus' day rather skated over this promise that God himself would be the Messiah. They just wanted a king who would kick out the Romans and put Israel back on the map.

This is why Jesus hushed up any idea that he was the expected king. He once asked his disciples who they thought he was. Peter answered, "You are the Messiah." Then Jesus ordered them, "Do not tell anyone about me."[2] He could see the crowds and riots and bloodshed if the idea took hold.

He didn't see himself as that sort of king. He allowed other Old Testament prophecies to mould his idea of Messiahship.

SERVANT

When Jesus was baptised, he publicly launched his ministry. God orchestrated the moment by sending the Holy Spirit to appear as a dove; and by speaking his own commentary.[3] "This is my own dear Son," he said, "with whom I am pleased."

It's a vitally important introduction to Jesus. And it shaped Jesus' own understanding of what he'd come to do.

The first half of God's words comes from one of the Messiah-king prophecies.[4] But the second half comes from a prophecy about a quite different figure: the Servant of the Lord.[5]

He was someone who would take his obedience to God all the way to suffering and even dying for him. The Jews of Jesus' day could see no possible connection between this Servant and the king they wanted.

But here's God saying they're one and the same person. Jesus is to be the Servant King who suffers and dies.

Still more. As Jesus thought about the Servant prophecies, he could see that his death would bear the punishment for our wrongdoing.

> ... because of our sins
> he was wounded,
> beaten because of the
> evil we did.
> We are healed by the
> punishment he
> suffered,
> made whole by the
> blows he received.[6]

He saw his death as the whole point of his life.[7]

SON OF MAN

But as he taught his disciples about his death, Jesus chose yet another Messiah-title for himself. He called himself the 'Son of Man'. This was the title he used most. In the Gospels we hear Jesus calling himself 'Son of Man' 53 times; but 'Son of David' only once — and even that was indirectly.[8]

The Son of Man first appeared in one of the visions of the Old Testament prophet Daniel. It was a glimpse into heaven at the end of time.

> He was approaching me,
> surrounded by clouds, and he
> went to the one who had been
> living for ever [i.e. God] and
> was presented to him. He was
> given authority, honour, and
> royal power, so that the people
> of all nations, races, and
> languages would serve him.
> His authority would last for
> ever, and his kingdom would
> never end.[9]

He was a 'power and glory' king, all right. But the time for his royal authority would not be till the next world.

This appealed to Jesus as an important correction to the way the Jews were thinking. And so did the title itself, with its stress on the Messiah's humanity.[10] Jesus was Son of Man as well as Son of God.

These are the strands of meaning woven into Jesus' teaching.

> ... the Son of Man did not come to be served; he came to serve and to give his life to redeem many people.[11]

The Messiah will not be a typical kingly ruler while on earth as a human being; all that will come later. In this life the Son of Man will be the Suffering Servant dying to pay the penalty for other people's sins.

CHRIST

Once Jesus had died, risen and returned to heaven, his followers didn't hesitate to call him the Messiah. Their Greek word for it was Christ. But it means exactly the same as the Hebrew Messiah — 'anointed', the person God has appointed to be king.

On the very day the Holy Spirit came to them, Peter was preaching, "this Jesus is the one that God has made Lord and *Messiah*!". And he told his hearers to be baptised in the name of Jesus *Christ*.[12]

The name stuck, and became, in effect, Jesus' surname. Within ten years his followers had become known not as Jesusites but as Christians. The letters from Paul and his team use this title for Jesus almost 400 times.

Jesus Christ — God's promised, prophesied, anointed King.

John explained the purpose of his Gospel like this:

> ... in order that you may believe that Jesus is the Messiah, the Son of God, and that through your faith in him you may have life.[13]

This is how Luke summed up the message of the first Christians:

> ... every day in the Temple and in people's homes they continued to teach adn preach the Good News about Jesus the Messiah.[14]

1   Isaiah 9:6,7.
2   Mark 8:29,30.
3   Matthew 3:16,17.
4   Psalm 2:7.
5   Isaiah 42:1. Isaiah foretold the Servant in four 'songs': 42:1-4; 49:1-6; 50:4-9; 52:13-53:12.
6   Isaiah 53:5.
7   John 12:23,24,27-33; 13:1.
8   Mark 12:35-37.
9   Daniel 7:13,14.
10 Good News Bible even translates the title in Daniel 7:13 "what looked like a human being".
11 Mark 10:45.
12 Acts 2:36,38.
13 John 20:31
14 Acts 5:42

3.9 "Why did God need to send His Son to die for us? Why didn't He just forgive us anyway?"

"Loony Judge lets scum off too lightly." "Teenage offender sentenced to holiday camp." "Life sentence should be FOR LIFE."

In recent years the British press and public have felt outrage again and again at the courts imposing lenient sentences for violent crime. Rapists, muggers and other armed robbers seem to leave prison before their victims have got over the trauma. And some young offenders seem to have a better time in detention than they would if they were free.

Why does this cause so much anger and distress? Because we feel it's unfair. They're getting away with murder, or near murder. Deep down we feel they should pay. Make up in some way for the damage they've done. The sense of justice is a deep human instinct.

FORGIVE AND FORGET?

Yet some people expect God just to write off our sins as if they didn't matter. And as if justice didn't matter. "God," they say, "shouldn't need to punish people. He should just forgive us. And, anyway, we haven't done anything too dreadful. I've certainly never murdered anyone or got a criminal record."

God shouldn't need to punish?! People are as soft on their own shortcomings as they say the courts are on crime. Have they even begun to understand who God is? He's the one and only totally just judge. His whole being sings with honesty, rightness and truth. He burns with the passion for justice.[1]

He sowed the longing for fairness and rights in us. He can't just flick his fingers and pretend we're paragons of virtue when we're not. The smallest unfairness makes him indignant and angry. Whenever we

tell a lie, we offend his concern for truth. Whenever we treat someone else as less important than ourselves, his instincts move him to defend them and put things right. When we cheat, we can be certain of one thing: he'll make sure we don't get away with it for ever.

That doesn't make him spiteful and unloving. It actually shows how much he loves us. His justice is love for the victims of *our in*justice. And it's the guarantee that he'll defend us when it's our turn to be victims.

WHY WE NEED JESUS

Don't let's kid ourselves. We all disqualified ourselves from heaven long ago. If God is total justice, only totally just people can live in his home. The first time we broke one of his laws we locked ourselves outside the door.

It's not just wrong things we may have done. Sin is also the good we have *not* done. Jesus said the most important of God's commandments was to love him with our whole heart, soul, mind and strength.[2] We may not be criminals; but we've all failed to keep this rule no. 1 in God's book. So we're all guilty of the greatest sin there is. Measured by this standard, none of us is 'better' than anyone else.

The only way we can get into heaven is to be proved innocent in God's court. But we're not innocent. So we must spend the rest of forever locked up in the prison of our own making. God may long to forgive us. But in all justice he can't.

Unless ...

Unless a totally just, faultless person could pay the fine for our wrongdoing. Take the punishment in our place. Remove the record of our sins.

That's who Jesus was. That's what he did for us on the cross. God was the Judge who sentenced us to death. But then he came in person to take the death sentence Himself. Only God Himself could with complete justice pay all the charges against us.

As Jesus died, he cried out with a loud shout[3], "My God, my God, why did you abandon me?" For the first time in eternity the umbilical cord which tied him in loving union to his Father was sliced in two. He went through every dreg of hell that we'd deserved. It cost him that much to be able to forgive us. A recent radio panel game asked the contestants which famous death in history they would like to have prevented. Rabbi Lionel Blue — the popular Jewish speaker — said "Jesus'". A kind thought. But a total misunderstanding. He would have chucked away the one key that can bring him (and all of us) into God's presence.

> Everyone has sinned and is far away from God's saving presence. But by the free gift of God's grace all are put right with him through Christ Jesus, who sets them free. God offered him, so that by his blood he should become the means by which people's sins are forgiven through their faith in him. God did this in order to demonstrate that he is righteous.[4]

Notes to page 79
1　See also 4.7 "How can I be sure the Holy Spirit is living in my life?" (page 98).
2　See also 4.6 "What's the Holy Spirit's job?" (page 96).
3　Romans 6:1,2.
4　1 John 1:9.

GOD'S SON

1　Psalm 11:4-7
2　Mark 12:28-30

3　Matthew 27:46
4　Romans 3:23-25.

3.10 "If we're forgiven by God, can we continue to do what's wrong?"

The incredible answer is that we *can* (but we shouldn't want to!). Jesus' death on the cross was deep enough to cover all the sins of the human race for all time. That means he paid the penalty for every wrong I'll ever commit — past, present and future. If I break God's law every day from now till I die, he can still forgive me. Jesus' death in my place was enough to make up even for as big a load of guilt as that. But … !

CHRISTIANS DON'T WANT TO SIN

There's a big difference from what we were like before we became Christians. We're now God's children. We have his Spirit living in us making us better people, making our characters gradually more like Jesus'.[1]

And because we're God's children, we should no longer *want* to go wrong. Because Jesus loves us so much, enough to take the full punishment for all our wrongdoing, we begin to love him in return. Would you be happy to punch your best friend's teeth in? That's the kind of way you'd hurt Jesus if you deliberately turned your back on living the way he wants you to. It's like siding with his executioners as they whipped his back and hammered nails into his hands and feet. The question we *should* be asking is, "If Jesus loves us like that, how can we go on doing wrong? And if we do, how can he go on loving us?"

WE CAN FIND FORGIVENESS WHEN WE DO SIN

We all continue to go wrong at times, even after we've become Christians and want to follow Jesus. We never reach perfection in this life, although God is steadily making us more like Jesus in the way we think and react and behave.[2]

He knows us through and through. He fully understands that when we slip up, it's usually without really meaning to. The moment we realise what we've done, we wish we hadn't. We may at times feel depressed at how slow we are to improve. But we never reach the end of his patience and forgiveness. Or even if we've deliberately let our love for Jesus grow cold, he's ready to take us back. He never stops loving us. We've only to say sorry, and at once he'll forgive us. He died for that sin as well.

So the best thing to do is: (1) tell Jesus atonce you're sorry. Don't let a strained silence grow up between you. It won't stop you being a Christian; but it'll stop you *feeling* like a Christian, and enjoying the close relationship you're meant to have with God. (2) Then get up and start following Jesus again. He's forgiven you, so don't mope around feeling bad about it.

Here's an interesting difference (one of many!) between pigs and sheep. If pigs fall in the mud, they roll around and wallow in it. If sheep fall in, they kick and struggle to get out and back on to firm ground as fast as possible. The Bible describes God's people as *sheep*, not as pigs! We still fall down from time to time, but God gives us the power not to stay there.

> Should we continue to live in sin so that God's grace will increase? Certainly not! We have died to sin — how then can we go on living in it?[3]
>
> But if we confess our sins to God, he will keep his promise and do what is right: he will forgive us our sins and purify us from all our wrongdoing.[4]

Footnotes - see page 78

3.11 "Where is Jesus now?"

People often say, "I'd find it easier to believe in Christianity if Jesus was still around. If we could go and hear him speak, and see him do some miracles." It's easy to see what they mean and agree with them.

But Jesus told his first followers it was actually *better* for them that he should go away. [1] What *can* he have meant?

MORE POWERFUL THAN HE WAS ON EARTH

First Jesus died and came back to life. For six weeks or so he reappeared to his friends and taught them. Then he went back to heaven. [2] He described it as returning to the glory he had with God in heaven before the world was made. [3]

In the Christian 'creeds' (or belief statements) we chart Jesus' present position as "sitting at God's right-hand side". In other words, He's God's right-hand man. Sitting on the throne, the most powerful place in the universe. Everything he came to do on earth is complete: mission successfully accomplished.

He's the King. And he always has been. He was the King when he was on earth, and he had great powers. But he also had limits. He was a human being. He needed time off to sleep and eat. He could only be in one place at a time; and listen to one person at a time.

Now he has no limits. He can see everywhere and hear everyone, all at once. He can do anything. And he wants to do it for us. He is our Brother in heaven.

But we're still on earth. Jesus has done everything needed before coming back to set up God's new heaven and earth. [4] But

for the moment he waits. This is the in-between time. There's still work for us to do on the old earth. Work that he doesn't leave us to do alone.

MORE PRESENT THAN HE WAS ON EARTH

Jesus said that although he was going away, he would come back to his followers. In a different form, which other people wouldn't be able to see. This isn't his final return to earth at the end of time; but an invisible coming, to Christians only. He'd been with those first Christians as a human being, another person *alongside* them. But now he would return as God's Spirit, a new presence *inside* them.

So we don't have to stand in a queue for him, waiting our turn. He's instantly available. We don't have to make a journey to where *he is*. He's with us where *we are*. We don't have to go through a vicar or Christian Union chairperson to get to him. He's with every single one of his people. So those who believe in him *can* hear him and see him at work. Just as much as when he was on earth as a man, if not more so. Only in a different, more spiritual way. [5]

---

1 John 16:7.
2 Acts 1:1-3,9.
3 John 17:5, quoted in the 'Bible box' overleaf.
4 See 7.8 "Will Jesus really come back?" (page 180).
5 For more on how Jesus makes himself real to us now, go to 4.2 "How does the Holy Spirit tie in with God and Jesus?" (page 88).

The night before he died Jesus prayed:

> Father! Give me glory in
> your presence now, the
> same glory I had with you
> before the world was
> made ... now I am
> coming to you; I am no
> longer in the world, but
> they are in the world ...
> May they be in us, just as
> you are in me and
> I am in you.[6]

And he told his followers:

> When I go, you will not
> be left all alone; I will
> come back to you ...
> Whoever loves me will
> obey my teaching. My
> Father will love him,
> and my Father and I
> will come to him and
> live with him.[7]

6 John 17:5, 11, 21
7 John 14:18,23

3.12 "What does it mean to 'know' Jesus and have him in your life?"

I sometimes talk about Christianity to groups of students. I usually ask them what they think being a Christian means. The commonest answers I get are:

(1) believing in God and Jesus;
(2) going to church;
(3) trying to follow Jesus' teaching.

These are certainly all things that Christians *do*. Jesus gives his followers truths to believe; a family of fellow)Christians to belong to; and a new lifestyle to guide our behaviour.

But none of them is the real heart of Christianity. They're not what *make* us Christians. It's possible to believe in our minds, belong outwardly and do our best to behave in a Christian way without being a real Christian at all.

KNOW GOD

Jesus says the heart of Christianity is to know God and have a personal relationship with him.[1] And as God makes himself known to us through Jesus, we can just as well call it getting to know *Jesus* and sharing our lives with *him*. And as the Holy Spirit actually makes the presence of Jesus real and vivid for us, we can also call it 'having the Holy Spirit in our lives'.

It's no longer me on my own, making my way through life. It's me and God — Jesus — the Holy Spirit. Jesus and me together.[2]

There was a man who became a Christian and suddenly understood what it really meant. His way of putting it was beautifully direct and fresh. "There *was* one of us," he said; "but *now* there's two of us."

Some people are aware straight-away that Jesus is with them, as an unseen but very real companion. Others have to start by taking it on trust. No two people have exactly the same experience. We are all refreshingly different. But the heart of the matter is, he promised to be with us; so we believe him and treat him as if he is.

So it becomes natural to talk to him. Not out loud necessarily. And not only in set prayer times. Any old time — the whole time!

We enjoy his friendship; share all our feelings with him, good and bad; thank him for the good things we see and experience; ask his help for the people we care for; for ourselves when we face the challenge of saying and doing the right thing; saying sorry to him when we get it wrong.

All this can happen when we're alone. But it's stronger and more natural still when we're with other Christians. That's why it's just about essential for Christians to meet together at least once a week. We strengthen each other in our relationship with Jesus.[3]

TURN AND BELIEVE

How exactly does this relationship start? Paul summed up what we need to do as "turn from our sins to God and believe in our Lord Jesus"[4]. Turn and believe. It's worth checking you've done this.

We need to make sure we've *turned*. Our natural instinct is to go our own way through life rather than God's. Following our own appetites and ambitions and choices, rather than doing what he wants. That's what the Bible calls sin. We can't be a Christian till we've turned round to go God's way.

We also need to make sure we've *believed*. In the Bible this means more than believing *that* Jesus is the Son of

God. It means putting our faith in him. Handing our lives over to him as boss — finding out his instructions for our lives — then relying on him to make us able to carry them out.

You probably know if your life's now facing God's way and following Jesus. But if you're not quite sure, why not make sure now? All you have to do is tell God you definitely want to turn and believe. You may have done it before, but there's no harm in saying it again.

If you'd like to put it into words, here's a prayer you could use:

Dear Father God,

My life has all too often gone my own way instead of yours. I want to turn it round to follow Jesus. Please come in on my life so that I know you and love you for myself. Amen.

> Jesus said:
> **Everyone whom my Father gives to me will come to me. I will never turn away anyone who comes to me...**[5]

When praying to his Father he said:

> **Eternal life means knowing you, the only true God, and knowing Jesus Christ, whom you sent.**[1]

1. How would you answer someone who says Jesus is not the only way to find God?
2. Some church leaders today say it isn't necessary to believe Jesus was really born from a virgin mother, came alive again after dying or ascended into heaven. Do you agree or disagree? Why?
3. What facts, qualities or stories about Jesus mean most to you at the moment (not more than three)? How would you use one of them to publicise Jesus in (a) a poster outside your church building; (b) a TV commercial?
4. How would you explain the heart of Christianity to a friend who is not a Christian?
5. How and when do you think you became committed to Christ? Did you realise this at the time, or only later? How would you tell the story to someone who is not a Christian?
6. What do you think Jesus wants to say now to (a) you; (b) your Christian fellowship group or church? What should you do about it?

---

1 John 17:3 (also in Bible box)
2 See 2.9 "How can God be one and three at the same time?" (page 50).

3 See 6.3 "Why is Church so boring?" (page 148).
4 Acts 20:21.
5 John 6:37.

What is the Holy Spirit?

Why do some people get so excited about the Holy Spirit?

Why doesn't the Holy Spirit heal everyone?

4

GOD'S SPIRIT

The Holy Spirit

4 GOD'S SPIRIT

4.1 "What is the Holy Spirit?"

What indeed! The English word Spirit is very hard to pin down. It usually means alcohol, the occult or a mood! As in wines and spirits; evil spirits; high spirits. So what might a holy spirit be?

People used to talk about the Holy Ghost, and you still find the name in some old hymns and songs. 'Ghost' was an old English word for spirit. These days, of course, it's positively misleading, because it has come to mean the paranormal appearance of a dead person. So what is the Holy Ghost or Spirit?

GOD'S BREATH

The point is, God is normally invisible to us on earth. We don't know what he looks like in his full glory in heaven. Our human eyes wouldn't be able to stand the sight in any case.[1] So God gives us glimpses or pictures (like signed photos) to help us understand him.

Jesus was a human picture. God made himself visible and showed us what he's like in the language we understand best — a human life.[2]

And Jesus told us to think of God as Father. That's a word picture which perfectly expresses God's relationship to us.[3]

Jesus used another word picture when he also called God "the Holy Spirit". In the Bible languages, Hebrew and Greek, the word 'Spirit' is the same as the words 'wind' and 'breath'; you can swap them for each other. In the Bible's record of the universe being created, it says "the Spirit of God was moving over the water".[4] But you could just as well talk of the Breath or Wind of God.

Now we're getting somewhere. Think about this: two basic proofs of whether a person's alive (or ever has been) are their breath and their children. Breath is the fundamental flicker of life — slap a baby to make it breathe; and if Granddad still wheezes, he's not dead! But once he is dead, his looks and his personality live on in sons and daughters.

So with God — he showed what he's like in his child Jesus; he shows he's alive in the world through his Spirit-Breath.

PERSONALISED BREATH

The Spirit is as much God as Jesus is. Like God and like the wind, he's everywhere; uncontrollable, but in control; invisible himself, but instantly visible in his effect on people. He turns crooks into carers and selfish people into sacrificial givers.

Like God as well, but unlike the wind, he's a person. 'He', not 'it'. John twice goes out of his way to stress this in his Greek version of Jesus' words. The Greek word for 'Spirit' is an 'it'; but John deliberately says 'he'.

> The Helper, the Holy Spirit, whom the Father will send in my name, *he* will teach you everything and make you remember all that I have told you.[5]
>
> When, however, the Spirit comes, who reveals the truth about God, *he* will lead you into all the truth … *he* will give me glory, because he will take what I say and tell it to you.[6]

John is usually a careful and correct writer. But here he blatantly breaks the rules of the Greek language. Who cares? God is greater than grammar. And John is taking words beyond their usual limits to tell us this all-important truth. The Holy Spirit is He — the Holy Spirit is God.

He's not just a force or a feeling, but the presence of God himself in the world. You can't see him, but he's as real as Jesus is. God made himself visible to us in Jesus; he makes himself present with us in his Spirit. He's present with Christians today just as surely as Jesus was with his first followers in first century Palestine.

Jesus promised that the Holy Spirit would come and remain in his followers:

> I will ask the Father, and he will give you another Helper, who will stay with you for ever. He is the Spirit … The world … cannot see him or know him. But you know him, because he remains with you and is in you.[7]

---

1 Exodus 33:18-23, especially 20.

2 John 1:18.

3 For more on God as Father, go to 2.5 "What's God like?" (page 42).

4 Genesis 1:2.

5 John 14:26. Good News Bible does not include the "he", but John's Greek does.

6 John 16:13,14.

7 John 14:16,17.

4.2 "How does the Holy Spirit tie in with God and Jesus?"

This puzzles a lot of people.

It's fairly easy to understand the Father-Son relationship between God and Jesus. But what's the link between the Spirit and either or both of them?

AT ONE WITH THEM

Jesus taught that the Holy Spirit had the closest imaginable relationship with himself. He told his first followers,

> I will ask the Father, and he will give you *another* Helper, who will stay with you for ever. He is the Spirit who reveals the truth about God.[1]

Jesus calls him 'another' Helper; but the word he used for 'another' means 'another one of exactly the same kind as me'. The only difference between them is that the Spirit will stay with Christians for ever, while Jesus was with the disciples on earth for no more than three years.

Jesus said some more about the Spirit:

> The world cannot receive him, because it cannot see him or know him. But you know him, because he remains with you and is in you. When I go, you will not be left all alone; *I* will come back to you.[2]

The Spirit is so like Jesus that Jesus can call him 'I'! This helps us see that the Holy Spirit is the presence of Jesus with all Christian people everywhere. The only difference between them here is that the Spirit is invisibly *inside* the life and experience of Christians, while Jesus on earth was *beside* them as another human being.

So the Spirit is the same God as Jesus. And as Jesus is the same God as the Father, so is the Spirit! Jesus made God visible to us while he was on earth; the Spirit now brings the Father and Jesus before our eyes. He's their invisible, spiritual presence living in us and with us.[3] He carries out their will on earth because he is the presence of God in the world.[4]

AT ONE WITH US

The Spirit is not only intimately linked with God and Jesus; he's intimately linked with us as well. He has replaced Jesus on earth, to do for all Christians today what Jesus did for his first followers.

Jesus was their friend — the Spirit is ours.

Jesus became their Lord — the Spirit must control our lives.

Jesus taught them — the Spirit teaches us.

Jesus healed them — the Spirit makes us more whole.

Jesus guarded them — the Spirit looks after us.

But because the Spirit is God-with-us in spiritual form, he does many of these things at a deeper, more spiritual level. Jesus had the natural limitations of a human being; so he could only be a close friend to a small number of his early followers. And even among them there was a circle of three and a circle of twelve he gave the most time and attention. But through his Spirit he offers non-stop, closer-than-close friendship to every single Christian in the world today.

In the same sort of way, most of Jesus' healings during his life on earth were visible and dramatic. He made sick people well and crippled people whole to show he was setting up God's kingdom on earth. But from the New Testament we learn that God's concern with us now is deeper still. He wants to "make us *holy in every way* and keep our *whole being* — spirit, soul, and body — *free from every fault*"![5] He does not achieve this in us by an instant word of command, but through a gradual, lifelong refining by his Spirit.[6]

The Holy Spirit always does these things in Jesus' name. He turns the spotlight away from himself and on to Jesus. So we're less aware of the Spirit than of Jesus. It's just as accurate and true to say that *Jesus* is our friend, Lord, teacher, healer and Saviour.

When well-known TV or radio personalities die, you hear some people saying, "I almost felt I knew them personally" or "They seemed more of a friend than just a name and a face".

With TV and radio it's a case of 'almost' and 'seemed'. With Jesus and God it's really true. The Holy Spirit enables us to know them personally. He brings them into our lives as a friend.

Jesus said about the Holy Spirit's relationship to himself:

> He will give me glory, because he will take what I say and tell it to you.[7]

Paul and Timothy said about the Holy Spirit's relationship to Christians:

> All of us, then, reflect the glory of the Lord with uncovered faces; and that same glory, coming from the Lord, who is the Spirit, transforms us into his likeness in an ever greater degree of glory.[8]

---

1 John 14:16,17.
2 John 14:17,18.
3 John 14:23.
4 See 4.1 "What is the Holy Spirit?" (page 86).
5 1 Thessalonians 5:23.
6 The image the New Testament uses to describe this process is fruit growing on a tree, which is a process of gradual, natural ripening. See Matthew 7:15-20; 12:33; 21:33,34,43; John 15:1-8,16, where Good News Bible translates as "fruit". But also Galatians 5:22,23; Ephesians 5:9; Philippians 1:11; Colossians 1:6,10; James 3:17; here the original writers wrote "fruit", but Good News Bible has used other words to explain the idea in English.
7 John 16:14.
8 2 Corinthians 3:18.

4.3 "What was the Holy Spirit doing *before* Jesus?"

God the Son doesn't come on to the Bible stage in person till the New Testament.

In the same way we don't get a full sight of God the Spirit till the New Testament. He's only given the name "Holy Spirit" three times in the Old Testament.[1] But all the same he is there, active in several important ways.

CREATING

God created the universe through his Spirit.

> The raging ocean that covered everything was engulfed in total darkness, and the Spirit of God was moving over the water.[2]

The word 'moving' was used of a mother-bird hovering or fluttering over her chicks, teaching them to fly.[3] The Spirit set the whole world pulsing, stirring, racing with life.

Although the Old Testament returns once or twice to the Spirit's part in making the world and keeping it in being[4], it's not a major theme. The Bible concentrates far more on the Spirit's work in God's people.

EMPOWERING

God's Spirit gave the rulers of the Israelites superhuman strength to defeat their enemies. Probably the most famous example is Samson.

> When he got to Lehi, the Philistines came running towards him, shouting at him. Suddenly the power of the LORD made him strong, and he broke the ropes round his arms and hands as if they were burnt thread. Then he found the jawbone of a donkey that had recently died. He bent down and picked it up, and killed a thousand men with it.[5]

It's typical of the Spirit's appearances in the Old Testament. The word in Hebrew is 'spirit', but Good News Bible translates as "the power of the LORD". This is fitting, because the Spirit's effect on Old Testament leaders is impersonal. Samson is made stronger, but not a better person. He remains a selfish, deceitful lout.

Another mark of the Spirit in the Old Testament heroes is that he comes and goes. From time to time Samson meets a crisis calling for special powers, and — zap! — the Spirit's upon him, hurling him on like a whirlwind. The Spirit is more *on* his people than *in* them. On — and then off again.

FORESEEING

It wasn't to be the Old Testament forever. The prophets looked forward to a better future for God's people. God foretold a new place and a new job for his Spirit in his people's lives.

> I will give you a new heart and a new mind. I will take away your stubborn heart of stone and give you an obedient heart. I will put my spirit in you and I will see to it that you follow my laws and keep all the commands I have given you.[6]

The Spirit will be 'in' the people, changing their nature. He'll make them obedient instead of stubborn; he'll give them the moral strength to keep God's laws. And this will be all God's people, not just the leaders. The prophet's looking over the wall into the New Testament.[7]

Through another prophet, Joel, God announces that under the new arrangements, even prophecy itself will no longer be limited to a select few.

> Afterwards I will pour out my Spirit on everyone: your sons and daughters will proclaim my message; your old people will have dreams, and your young people will see visions. At that time I will pour out my Spirit even on servants, both men and women.[8]

---

1 Psalm 51:11; Isaiah 63:10,11.
2 Genesis 1:2.
3 Deuteronomy 32:11.
4 Job 26:13; Psalm 104:30.
5 Judges 15:14,15. Compare 13:25; 14:6,19.
6 Ezekiel 36:26,27.
7 Jeremiah 31:31-34. The Holy Spirit was 'inspiring' and overseeing the whole Old Testament as people wrote it. See 5.5 "Why the Bible rather than any other books?" (page 122).
8 Joel 2:28,29. Peter understood the coming of the Holy Spirit on the Day of Pentecost as the beginning of the prophecy's fulfilment (Acts 2:16-21).

4.4 "Why do we only seem to find out about the Holy Spirit after we become Christians?"

Mainly because the Holy Spirit doesn't draw attention to himself. He's the unseen, background member of God's three-in-one. He wants to give the limelight to the Father and most of all to Jesus.[1]

So when Christians talk to other people about Christianity, they talk about Jesus. When we first look into the Christian faith — and when we first become Christians — Jesus fills the whole horizon.

This is just how it should be. The Holy Spirit is making sure it happens this way. He's like the night-time floodlighting you often see on historic buildings. It's incredibly powerful and well focused. But we don't stand there saying, "What a beautiful floodlight!" We say, "What an amazing castle — or cathedral — or statue!" The Holy Spirit lights up Jesus.

We are often not aware of the Holy Spirit till later. But he's fully involved in every stage of introducing us to Jesus.

HE PROVES US WRONG

If at one stage we weren't Christians, he was hard at work bringing that stage to an end! Jesus explains it like this.

> When he [the Holy Spirit] comes, he will prove to the people of the world that they are wrong about sin and about what is right and about God's judgement.[2]

We can't move from being 'non-Christians' to Christians without learning that we were wrong. Wrong in not worshipping Jesus as God. Wrong in not keeping God's laws. Wrong in thinking it didn't matter.

How do we reach this point of being ready to turn round from the wrong direction we've been living our lives in? It feels to us as if we simply change our minds. But why do we change our minds? According to Jesus, it's not because we work it out or Christians persuade us. At least, that's not the heart of what is going on.

Jesus says the real reason is, the Holy Spirit proves it to us. With some of us he simply convinces our minds; with others he stirs a deep inner conflict which only finds relief in coming to terms with Jesus. Either way, the Holy Spirit's so powerful, he makes sure it happens. But he's so nimble-fingered, we don't even realise he's there.

HE GIVES US A SECOND START

The Holy Spirit doesn't just do the hatchet job of proving us wrong. He lifts us up and puts us right. Here's Jesus' mysterious way of explaining what happens.

> I am telling you the truth: no one can see the Kingdom of God without being born again.[3]

They didn't know what he meant, so he spelt it out again.

> No one can enter the Kingdom of God without being born of water and the Spirit.[4]

We start life on earth by being born physically. But we can't start life in God's Kingdom till we're 'born' a second time. Born spiritually into God's family.

And this doesn't happen because we make up our minds to be Christians. It's done to us through "water and the Spirit".

The Holy Spirit brings us to the point where we say, "I've been all wrong. I need to be washed clean. I need to start life again with God's help."

When we reach out to God with that need and that cry for help, he answers — through his Spirit. He washes us all through, and gives us a fresh start in life. We've been born all over again.[5] The Holy Spirit's like the 'mother' who bears us through the long months of preparation. And then like the 'midwife' who brings us — often kicking and struggling — into the new, eternal life of heaven.

We didn't make the first move at all. It was all the Holy Spirit's doing. But in the same way as when we were born physically, we had little clue what was happening to us at the time. We only came to understand it later.

And even then the Holy Spirit was still unobtrusively at work. He was the 'nurse' or 'tutor' telling us what family we belong to.

> … by the Spirit's power we cry out to God, "Father! my Father!" God's Spirit joins himself to our spirits to declare that we are God's children.[6]

Perhaps you've had that sense of being closely related to God. He's your Father! Jesus is your brother! You're one of the family! When you feel that way, it's the Holy Spirit joining himself to your spirit.

But once again, he doesn't draw attention to himself. He makes you aware of Jesus and the Father.

---

1 John 16:13-14. There is an interesting case of this in Acts 19. Paul meets some new, but very uninstructed, Christian disciples. They had never heard of the Holy Spirit (verse 2). Paul proceeds to teach them — not about the Holy Spirit, but about Jesus (verses 4,5).

2 John 16:8.

3 John 3:3.

4 John 3:5.

5 This is simply saying in other words how we become Christians. For what may be a more familiar way of putting it, go to 3.12 "What does it mean to 'know' Jesus?" (page 82).

6 Romans 8:15,16.

4.5 "Why do some people get so excited about the Holy Spirit?"

Lots of reasons.

Sometimes it's simply because they haven't heard about him or didn't understand him before.[1] Suddenly they discover a whole new side to God they'd never dreamed of. Delia Smith the TV cook says she was a Christian for three years before she took in that she could have a personal relationship with Jesus through the Spirit. If you've never seen that God's actually with us as a living presence to strengthen and comfort us, the new discovery will transform your whole life!

There are several other sides of God which the Holy Spirit may bring home to us because he stands for them in a special way. I find them all exciting.

● SPIRITUAL

Sooner or later we see through the world's tendency to value everything by what it costs. We discover the best things in life are not things at all! They're price-less because you can't buy them: people, relationships, qualities, God himself. Our deepest needs are spiritual. And the Holy Spirit's there to meet them.

● SUPERNATURAL

The scientifically advanced world we live in likes to have a rational explanation for everything. This can affect us as Christians and make us expect pitifully little in answer to our prayers. We can easily forget that God isn't limited by the natural processes of the world he made. On occasion he may choose to override them.

Of course the Holy Spirit is no *more* supernatural than the Father or Jesus. But his dramatic entry among the first Christians on the Day of Pentecost announced a supernatural God in the grand manner.[2] He filled the house with the roar of a force 17 hurricane; that should blow the cobwebs off our feeble

faith. He sparked off a trail of flame which lit up everyone in the room like a neon sign; our lives are meant to blaze out the name of Jesus in bright lights. He set their tongues wagging in foreign languages; he'll enable us to take the Good News of Jesus to every race and nation under the sun.

● AWE-INSPIRING

Again, the Spirit's no more mysterious or awesome than the Father who loves us enough to adopt us, or the Son who becomes a human being to die for us. But we can become over-familiar with them. We can begin to cut them down to our own size.

The Holy Spirit does well to remind us that God is infinitely greater than us. He's frightening as well as loving. In the early days of the Christian Church he caused the death of a couple who thought they could deceive him; and blinded a magician who tried to block the spread of the Good News.[3] He's not to be ignored or played around with.

Remember that one of the Spirit's other names is Wind.[4] The wind's a mysterious, awesome thing. It can be a devastating tornado, as well as a gentle breeze.

● SPEAKING

God doesn't leave us to muddle through life unguided. He communicates with us, Spirit to spirit. The Holy Spirit is the talking God.

He speaks to us through every evidence of God's craftsmanship in the world all round us. Through our conscience or reasoning or other inner nudges when we pray about the right thing to do. Through what other people say to us — whether they're friends chatting or giving advice, or Christian speakers and writers bringing God's word to us. All of these can be the mouthpiece for the Spirit's voice.

But his main way of speaking to us is through the Bible. He 'inSpired' the original writers; now he wants to bring their message home to us.[5] The Bible's the 'spiritual milk' we need to help us grow as Christians.[6] When I come to understand what something in the Bible means, or what God's wanting me to do about it, I'm incredibly excited. Almost as excited as when someone I've prayed for becomes a Christian. God's not only talking to them; he's talking to me!

● LEADING

It's possible to think (wrongly) of the Father only being in heaven; and Jesus only being in the past. God the Spirit puts us right: he's here and now, taking hold of our lives. He's God's Breath.[7] If I burn my finger, I blow on it to cool it down. If a wasp lands on it, I blow to frighten the danger away. In the same way God's Breath comforts the disturbed; but also disturbs the over-comfortable. Whichever you are, there's a loving wind blowing that won't let you stagnate. Don't resist him, restrain him, make him sad.[8]

He's the impact of Jesus on you; and he wants to sweep you up into doing what Jesus wants. Let him lead you and fill you.[9] Sometimes he carries us along gently like the sea breeze on top of a cliff. But sometimes he blows us right off our feet.

SPIRITUS
I used to think of you
as a symphony
neatly structured,
full of no surprises.
Now I see you as
a saxophone solo
blowing wildly
into the night,
a tongue of fire,
flicking in unrepeated
          patterns.
                    Steve Turner*

* Steve Turner, *Up to Date* (Hodder and Stoughton, 1983) p.166.

That's Someone worth getting excited about.

The early Christians found the Holy Spirit blowing and driving them out to tell the world about Jesus:

When they finished praying, the place where they were meeting was shaken. They were all filled with the Holy Spirit and began to proclaim God's message with boldness.[10]

The Holy Spirit said to Philip,

"Go over to that carriage [of an Ethiopian official] and stay close to it." … Then Philip … told him the Good News about Jesus.[11]

1 See 4.4 "Why do we only seem to find out about the Holy Spirit after we become Christians?" (page 92).

2 Acts 2:1-13.

3 Acts 5:1-11; 13:8-12. It is worth noting that these supernatural judgments (life to death and sight to blindness) were the exact reverse of Jesus' miracles (see 3.6 "Can we really believe in Jesus' miracles?" (page 70)); the Holy Spirit is not wholly predictable. He is full of surprises.

4 See 4.1 "What is the Holy Spirit?" (page 86).

5 2 Timothy 3:16; 2 Peter 1:21. See 5.3 "How does God 'speak' through the Bible?" (page 118).

6 1 Peter 2:2.

7 See 4.1 "What is the Holy Spirit?" (page 86).

8 Acts 7:51; 1 Thessalonians 5:19; Ephesians 4:30.

9 Galatians 5:16,25; Ephesians 5:18. For more on what this means, go to 4.8 "What do people mean by being 'renewed in the Spirit'?" (page 100).

10 Acts 4:31.

11 Acts 8:29,35.

4.6 "What's the Holy Spirit trying to do to me?"

Loads! And it's all good. So don't get nervous.

The basic answer is, he's setting up home inside you. When Jesus promises to be with his followers, he actually makes himself present in the invisible form of his Spirit. The Holy Spirit *is* Jesus and the Father with us and in us.[1]

Liverpool football supporters chant "You'll never walk alone". It's literally true for Christians. The Holy Spirit's always with us. Wherever we go — home, work, spare time, fun, danger — he's there. We never walk, run, drive, dive, fly, stand, sit, sleep alone. We can enjoy his company and draw on his strength any time we need to.

What's more, we're the Holy Spirit's *permanent* address. Once he's moved in, he has no plans to move out again. He's a Breath and a foretaste of heaven. He's entered our lives *for ever*. The New Testament describes him as God's name-label or 'stamp of ownership' on us; he's God's guarantee that we really belong to him and are on our way to a fuller experience of him in heaven.[2]

TEMPLE

But the New Testament doesn't allow us to domesticate the Holy Spirit. It uses a breathtaking idea to explain what he's doing. It describes Christians as the *temple* of the Holy Spirit. In the Old Testament the temple was the place where people could find God's presence and worship him. The Spirit who lives in us isn't a cosy feeling but Almighty God. And each and every Christian has taken over from the Jerusalem temple as the place on earth where God chooses to live.

We should take time to let this sink in. Our whole life is a time and place of worship. You don't have to wait till Sunday to meet God. He's with you all the time. Everything you do can be shared with him and offered to him as a way of showing your love.

But this is also a challenging truth. The temple, as God's home, was meant to be a place of spotless purity. So any abuse of our bodies is fouling up the temple. Too much drink or drugs, too much work and no sleep, sex outside marriage[3] — all are misusing God's home. If he's with us, he hears us rubbish other people or tell them lies. He feels our selfish thoughts and they stab him. He wants to clean us up and teach us to put his wishes before our own. He's the new owner.

When we first become Christians, none of us is remotely fit to be God's house. Our lives are more like a tumbledown shack than a gleaming temple. But the Holy Spirit sets about a lifelong programme of renovations. Bit by bit he makes our characters more like Jesus.[4] We steadily become people where Jesus feels at home.

All this interior rebuilding isn't just for our comfort and convenience. It's to bring glory to Jesus. The Jerusalem temple reflected something of the love and praise God's people felt for him. Now our lives are to do the same. They're to be an advert recommending Jesus to others. Once again, this is something we'd make a complete hash of on our own. But the Holy Spirit's with us to do the attracting through us. He makes us able to be a good plug for Jesus.[5]

TOGETHER

What's true of you as a Christian on your own is all the more powerfully true when you meet other Christians. The temple's a meeting-place for all God's people. The

Holy Spirit lives in your fellowship — your sharing together and caring for each other. He wants to deepen and refine your time together as much as your time on your own.[6]

Paul teaches that every Christian and the whole Church are both the Spirit's temple. First, he speaks to the Church as a whole.

> Surely you know that you are God's temple and that God's Spirit lives in you![7]

Then he addresses each church member.

> Don't you know that your body is the temple of the Holy Spirit, who lives in you and who was given to you by God? You do not belong to yourselves but to God; he bought you for a price. So use your bodies for God's glory.[8]

---

1 See 4.2 "How does the Holy Spirit tie in with God and Jesus?" (page 88).

2 2 Corinthians 1:22; Ephesians 1:13,14.

3 If you don't think of sex outside marriage as misuse, go to 1.4 "You don't have to get married to live with someone" (page 18).

4 See 4.7 "How can I be sure the Holy Spirit's living in my life?" (page 98).

5 Acts 1:8. See also 4.9 "What are the 'gifts' of the Holy Spirit?" (page 103).

6 See 4.11 "How can I be sure the Holy Spirit's at work in my church?" (page 108).

7 1 Corinthians 3:16. — 8 1Cor. 6:19,20.

* From *Family Worship* (Church Pastoral Aid Society, 1971), p.7.

4.7 "How can I be sure the Holy Spirit's living in my life?"

The short answer is: because he says he is. Jesus has promised to be with all his followers in the form of his Spirit.[1] This is the 'inside story' of what happens when we become Christians. We can trust Jesus' promise because he's completely reliable, even at times when we don't *feel* as if he's with us.

But there's also a simple, practical test we can take. How holy are we?

HOLY

He's the *Holy* Spirit. His job's not just to share life with us, but to make us holy too. He's here to make us like himself.

Don't run away. The word 'holy' has a bad image. People think it means solemn, unsmiling and religious. Not a bit of it.

Even the English word 'holy' means something good and positive. It means *healthy*. It's related to the word whole. Where we were broken, the Spirit wants to mend us. Where we were mixed up, he wants to sort us out. Where we were dirty, he wants to make us clean. Where we were weak, he wants to make us strong.

But the word 'holy' in the Bible is based on Old Testament Hebrew. And there it means *different*. Set apart from the ordinary because we belong to another sphere of reality. God calls us as Christians to belong to him and be like him. Our first loyalty is to *God's* family, rather than any other human family. And God's 'family likeness' shows. The 'Holy' Spirit (the 'Something Else' Spirit, the Godlike Spirit) makes us different too; he makes us grow more like Jesus.

GODLIKE

If this idea sounds a bit airy-fairy, Paul puts flesh on it. He gives a list of the ways the Spirit is wanting to make every Christian's character different — and better.

> The Spirit produces love, joy, peace, patience, kindness, goodness, faithfulness, humility and self-control.[2]

That's the kind of person who's holy. If at first it sounds a bit weak and pathetic, you need to think again. The world around us thinks love, peace, humility, etc. are slushy or wishy-washy. But that just shows how *different* God's holiness is.

Loving unlovely people without giving up on them is incredibly tough and strong. Joy is being able to live life to the full, without regret or other negative feelings. Peace doesn't mean being an unassertive doormat; it means overcoming conflict, resolving it, holding it at bay in the future. Kindness, goodness, faithfulness, humility are qualities it may be fashionable to sneer at. But when you come across them in other people, they make the world a better place. They take real strength of character to achieve.

The last quality in the list — self-control — is perhaps the most surprising and revealing of all. It doesn't mean a negative, killjoy spirit of giving up more and more things for Lent. It's the growing ability to control and master that most destructive wild animal in the world — yourself!

The glorious mystery is that as you ask God's Spirit to be more in control of your life, you become more in control of it yourself, not less! You don't turn into a mindless, bloodless robot, twitching and marching as God twiddles the controls. You become a responsible human being, making your own decisions — but tuned in to what God wants. You gradually become the person *you* want to be, because that's the person *God* wants you to be.

Paul's list of Holy Spirit character-marks is the one test the Bible gives to show whether we've got the Spirit living in us or not. Some people get excited by miracles or speaking in foreign languages. "That proves I've got the Spirit!" But they're confusing what the Holy Spirit may do *sometimes* in *some* of us with what he wants to do in *all* of us *all* the time.[3]

YOU?

As you look back over the time you've been a Christian, can you see some change towards these marks of God's character? In all honesty, are you growing a little more patient, kind or reliable than you once were?

Yes? Then thank God, because he's clearly at work in your life. You couldn't make those changes on your own.

But if not — if you're no closer to Jesus' love, joy, peace, goodness or self-control than you ever were — then you've hardly begun to grow as a Christian, however loud you may sing at church meetings! You've got a whole lifetime of excitement ahead of you — and of hard, determined uphill climbing.

For growing holy *is* a lifetime's job. We'll never reach the end of it on earth. And it's a seven-day-a-week job, with every waking hour of every day written into the contract. It's a good thing the Holy Spirit's working at it with you. You'd have no hope of keeping it up on your own.

Paul reminds us that growing holy is not something we sit back and let happen automatically. The Holy Spirit leads us to work at it.

So then, my brothers and sisters, we have an obligation, but it is not to live as our human nature wants us to. For if you live according to your human nature, you are going to die; but if by the Spirit you put to death your sinful actions, you will live. Those who are led by God's Spirit are God's children.[4]

---

1 John 14:16,17,23. See also 3.12 "What does it mean to 'know' Jesus and have him in your life?" (page 82) and 4.6 "What's the Holy Spirit trying to do to me?" (page 96).

2 Galatians 5:22,23.

3 Miracles and speaking in tongues are two of the 'gifts' of the Holy Spirit — all Christians have different gifts. Love, joy, peace, etc. are part of what some Bible translations call the 'fruit' of the Spirit. All Christians should show the same fruit. See also 4.9 "What are the 'gifts' of the Holy Spirit?" (page 103).

4 Romans 8:12-14.

4.8 "What do people mean by being 'renewed in the Spirit'?"

I'd like to think they meant what the New Testament means. But I'm not sure all of them do.

RENEWED

The word 'renew' appears only twice in the Good News Bible New Testament. Neither talks of being renewed 'in the Spirit'. But both make clear what sort of renewal they mean, and the part the Holy Spirit plays in it.

1. Everybody has an inner, 'spiritual being' which isn't the same as their physical body. The body gradually decays and dies; but for Christians the spirit has come alive, and it becomes gradually stronger as it grows towards its real home in eternity.

> Even though our physical being is gradually decaying, yet our spiritual being is renewed day after day.[1]

2. The second passage talks entirely about this inner 'spiritual being'. It's not the 'old self' we had before we started as Christians, which had a habit of lying and living only for itself. It's the Christian's "new self or being" which is gradually coming to know God.

> Do not lie to one another, for you have taken off the old self with its habits and have put on the new self. This is the new being which God, its Creator, is constantly renewing in his own image, in order to bring you to a full knowledge of himself.[2]

The new spiritual being at the heart of every Christian is *renewed every day*. We receive fresh spiritual life and strength as we grow constantly more like God (or "in his image"). And the source of this daily renewal is God the Creator, working as always through his Spirit.

There is, though, a third passage where the New Testament's original Greek *does* talk about us being "renewed in the Spirit". But the Good News Bible translates it (perfectly fairly) as "the Holy Spirit gives us new life".

> God ... saved us, through the Holy Spirit, who gives us new birth and new life by washing us.[3]

This is the beginning of the story. When we become Christians, the Spirit *renews* us. He washes us clean of our sins, and gives us a whole new start in life. It's like being born all over again.[4]

So we can sum up what the New Testament says about being "renewed in the Spirit" as:

(1) The Holy Spirit makes us completely new when we become Christians. He gives us a new being by bringing our spirit alive with eternal life.

(2) He sustains and deepens that new life every day from then on. He helps us to know God better and prepares us for heaven.

But some people talk about being "renewed in the Spirit" as if they'd met the Holy Spirit in some completely new and different way some time after they started as Christians.

It sounds much the same as the

meaning some Christians give to being "baptised in the Spirit". They talk of it as an experience which happens after they've become Christians. Here again I think they're disagreeing with the New Testament.

BAPTISED

The expression "baptised in the Spirit" comes only seven times in the New Testament (and none at all in the Old). Four of the seven refer to the same event: the four Gospels all record John the Baptist announcing that while *he* baptised people with water, *Jesus* would baptise with the Holy Spirit.[5]

The next two of the seven references come in Acts, and they too refer to just one event. Shortly before he went back to heaven, Jesus told his apostles they'd be baptised with the Spirit a few days later. It's clear he means the Day of Pentecost, when the Spirit burst upon them with the sound of wind and the appearance of fire.[6]

The last mention comes from Paul when he tells the Corinthians:

> Christ is like a single body, which has many parts; it is still one body, even though it is made up of different parts. In the same way, all of us, whether Jews or Gentiles, whether slaves or free, *have been baptized into the one body by the same Spirit, and we have all been given the one Spirit to drink.*[7]

In other words, it wasn't just the apostles on the Day of Pentecost. *All* Christians belong to Christ's body. So *all* Christians have been baptised by the Spirit. You can't *be* a Christian without the Holy Spirit.

One reason for the confusion is that people treat different Bible descriptions of becoming a Christian as if they meant different things. The New Testament talks about "following Jesus", "being born again", "being converted", "believing (or putting your faith) in Jesus", "receiving eternal life". All express different sides of becoming a Christian.

"Being baptised in the Spirit" (or "renewed in the Spirit") is another. "Baptise" means to wet or soak, anywhere from a few drops to a drowning. Before we become Christians, we're spiritually both dirty and dry; an infected area and a desert. When God's Spirit comes in on our lives — at the very moment we become Christians — he washes and waters us, making us alive to God.

That is what the ceremony of baptism pictures. The minister sprinkles or submerges the new Christian with *water*. But that's just an outward way of showing that Jesus floods them with *his Spirit*.

(continued overleaf)

---

1 2 Corinthians 4:16.

2 Colossians 3:9,10.

3 Titus 3:4,5.

4 For more on this, go to 4.4 "Why do we only seem to find out about the Holy Spirit after we become Christians?" (page 92).

5 Matthew 3:11; Mark 1:8; Luke 3:16; John 1:33.

6 Acts 1:5; 2:1-4; 11:16. For more about the meaning of Pentecost, go to 4.5 "Why do some people get so excited about the Holy Spirit?" (page 94).

7 1 Corinthians 12:12,13.

So it's a mistake to say that any Christian hasn't been baptised (or renewed) in the Spirit.[1]

FILLED

I don't question the experience of Christians who say they've been baptised or renewed in the Spirit *after* becoming Christians — just the way they describe it. I think they'd be truer to the New Testament to say they've been *filled* with the Spirit.

For Paul not only said that God has given us the Spirit to drink. He also said, "be *filled* with the Spirit".[2] Don't just take a sip; knock your head back. Not just a liqueur glass — have a barrel!

We're only baptised once. But the Holy Spirit wants to *go on* filling us ever after. We should be filled afresh with the Spirit every day of our lives.

Again, this is not some different experience from being full of *Jesus*. It's simply another expression for the same thing. The Holy Spirit *is* the Spirit of Jesus. So being filled with the Spirit is handing over afresh to Jesus the control of every part of our lives.

I pray, "Lord Jesus, please fill me again with your Spirit", as soon as I wake up each morning. I recommend it as a good prayer to pray regularly.

---

1 Of course, there are some people who *think* they are Christians, but are not really. They call themselves Christians but have never submitted to Jesus in repentance and faith. It would be true to say that *they* have not been baptised in the Spirit, even if they have been baptised in water. But they should not be confused with real Christians, who *have* been baptised in the Spirit, even if they have *not* yet been baptised in water! See also 6.8 "What are baptism and communion all about?" (page 159).

2 Ephesians 5:18.

KISS OF HEAVEN

How the Archbishop of Canterbury was filled afresh with the Holy Spirit.

George Carey became a Christian when he was 17. Twenty years later he was teaching in a Bible college but was upset by his lack of spirituality.

Then on a visit to Canada, just before he was due to preach in Toronto, he unexpectedly found himself on his knees. He confessed to God that he had been so busy in serving him that he had somehow lost him. He asked to be filled again with God's Spirit. He knew that without this he could not go on.

Nothing special happened immediately after this except that he kept hearing the word *Shamayim* repeated. It is the Hebrew word for "heaven". Later he understood that what he had experienced that evening was a foretaste of heaven as the Holy Spirit became so real to him.

He felt that this experience was a turning point in his life as a Christian. Dying embers had been fanned by God's Spirit into a fire. He could now move on again.*

---

*   Adapted from Robert Backhouse, *Invaded by Love* (Marshall Pickering, 1993), pp.58,59.

4.9 "What are the 'gifts' of the Holy Spirit?"

The word the Bible uses for spiritual *gifts* is the same word as Christmas or birthday *presents*. It's a lovely idea — God showers his children with prezzies!

The fullest passage of teaching about them in the New Testament is 1 Corinthians 12.

> There are different kinds of spiritual gifts, but the same Spirit gives them. There are different ways of serving, but the same Lord is served. There are different abilities to perform service, but the same God gives ability to all for their particular service. The Spirit's presence is shown in some way in each person for the good of all.[1]

Paul thinks what he's saying is so important that the first three sentences say it over and over again in slightly different ways. This helps the points he's making to get through, even to thick heads like ours.

1. God gives the gifts — so there's no room for us to be proud about them. When you tell someone they're a 'gifted' singer or footballer, they often take it as praise or admiring their efforts. But the very word 'gifted' means their talent or skill isn't their own invention; someone gave it to them. And that someone is, of course, the God who made them. He's the author of natural ability in eye and foot and voice, as much as he is of the gifts of spirit mentioned in this chapter. When we use them, it's not us being clever; it's God working with us and through us.

And Paul stresses that it's the whole three-in-one God working together. "The same Spirit ... the same Lord [Jesus] ... the same God ... " Some people think you only find 'the gifts' among Christians who talk a lot about the Holy Spirit. But Paul won't let us split God up in this way. The gifts come from Father, Son *and* Spirit.

2. God gives to all Christians. Paul says God gives ability "*to all*", and the Spirit's presence is shown in "*each person*" in the Church. Many of us feel inferior to others, and jealous of their gifts. But in fact nobody's left out, or 'ungifted', or second best. None of us is 'better' than anyone else; we just have different gifts.

3. The gifts enable us to serve. God's presents are not for secret hoarding or for showing off. They're "abilities to perform service". They should be hard work! They're "the Spirit's presence" in us "for the good of all". They're not for our own benefit but for the rest of the church.

So they're not an ego trip to give us a warm glow or an adoring fan club. They're God's way of giving us a firm push and saying, "Get out there and do something to help the others. Build them up in their faith or their church life. Work together with them at the job I've given you all to do."

WHAT ARE THE GIFTS?

In 1 Corinthians 12, Paul lists apostles, prophets and teachers; speaking God's message, often marked by special wisdom or knowledge; faith; power to work miracles and to heal; the ability to tell the difference between gifts that come from the Spirit and those that don't; speaking in a language we've never learnt, or translating someone else as they do so; helping others and leading them.[2]

(continued overleaf)

---

1 1 Corinthians 12:4-7.
2 1 Corinthians 12:8-10,28.

Obviously miracles or suddenly being able to speak in a foreign language (without lessons!) sound very exciting, and some people talk as if these were the *only* gifts of the Spirit. And because these gifts seem 'supernatural', the same people are apt to think this is the proof God really is with them and working in them.

But healing miracles and 'speaking in strange tongues' also happen in other religions, and even in some non-religious groups. They're not in themselves evidence of the Holy Spirit's presence.[1] Nor of course, even when they *are* inspired by the Holy Spirit, are they his only gifts. Many of his other ways of working through us are much more 'normal' or ordinary activities — like teaching, helping or leading.

It's best to think of them all as ways God wants us to serve him and other people. God gives us all one or more of these abilities. They *can* be used selfishly. But when our motive is to do what God wants and help others, our gifts hit the spiritual jackpot. They've an uncanny knack of making people realise God is with them, so they want to praise him.

Paul doesn't suggest for a moment that his list in 1 Corinthians 12 is *all* the spiritual gifts. In other places he mentions encouraging, giving, kindness, evangelism, reading the Bible aloud, preaching and pastoral care. He includes dangerous experiences like martyrdom or being rescued from it; and states of life such as being single or married, or simply being a Christian.[2] All are gifts the Holy Spirit can equip us to accept and use for God.

And aren't there others again, which the New Testament doesn't mention as such? Engineering, architecture, building maintenance, electrics, music, drama, dance, artwork, flower growing and arranging, cooking, being good with words or figures or children … I've seen them all doing God's work. You've probably seen others again.

WHAT ARE YOUR GIFTS?

You may already have a clear idea. But on the other hand, you may not. You may have had difficulty finding employment. This can be deeply depressing, and can leave you feeling useless. But none of us is useless to God. If you're a Christian he's certainly given you one or more special gifts for serving him and building up the church. It's not humble to say "I'm no good at anything"; it's disbelieving God.

The way to find out what our gift(s) might be is simply to ask, and then get on with whatever opportunities open up. Ask God to show you and use you. Ask others what they think you're good at. Offer to help your church and any other Christian fellowship you belong to. If you don't, they'll miss out.

It may only be in very small, humdrum ways at first. Your gift(s) may not be what you expected or even what you'd have chosen for yourself. But as you serve Jesus and his people, the special abilities God's given you will begin to grow and become clear.[3]

Each one, as a good manager of God's different gifts, must use for the good of others the special gift he has received from God. Whoever preaches must preach God's messages; whoever serves must serve with the strength that God gives, so that in all things praise may be given to God through Jesus Christ … [4]

1 The New Testament 'proof' of the Spirit's presence is a holy character like Jesus'. See 4.7 "How can I be sure the Holy Spirit's living in my life?" (page 98).

2 Romans 12:8; Ephesians 4:11; 1 Timothy 4:13,14; 1 Corinthians 13:3; 2 Corinthians 1:10,11; 1 Corinthians 7:7; Romans 6:23.

3 For more about this, see 6.1 "You can be a Christian without going to church (page 144).

4 1 Peter 4:10,11.

4.10 "Why doesn't the Holy Spirit heal everyone who's ill?"

David Watson was a widely known and much loved English preacher in the 1970s and 1980s. When he was 50 he developed cancer. He received both surgery and prayer for miraculous healing. Many felt it unthinkable that he should die when God was using him so exceptionally. Churches throughout the world prayed for his healing with an urgency and a persistence I've never seen matched. Yet almost a year after the illness was diagnosed, David died. Many were left asking "Why?"

Only God knows the full answer, of course. But the Bible gives us a number of pointers to help us get our bearings.

SUPERNATURAL HEALING?

Without a doubt, the Holy Spirit can perform miracles as much as Jesus could. God is well able to heal people at 'heaven-speed' (i.e. instantly, or abnormally fast) rather than at 'earth-speed' (i.e. gradually), and he sometimes does.

But God nowhere promises to heal everybody (or even all Christians) miraculously.[1] So while God would encourage us to pray for it, we can't demand it.

When someone's not healed miraculously, it's because God chooses not to work that way. He's in charge, and it's entirely up to him to decide how he'll answer our prayers. When people have prayed in vain for a miraculous healing, they're understandably disappointed. And sometimes their disappointment makes them look round for someone to 'blame'. They feel it would be unChristian to blame God. So tragically they blame themselves — or worse still, the sufferer — for not having enough faith.

They're quite wrong to do this. God takes full responsibility for what he does. So if anyone is 'to blame', it is indeed him.

But of course blame's the wrong word. It suggests someone's done something wrong. But no-one has. They prayed, which was good. God heard, and answered their prayer in a different way, which is also good. We can't see the whole picture as he can. We have to trust that the answer he gives us is better than the one we asked for.

NATURAL HEALING?

What *is* wrong is a feeling that sometimes creeps in that God's *only* involved if there's a miracle. This is a faulty way of thinking our modern world can lead us into. Because science can explain so much of how the world's natural processes work, we can slip into thinking they have a life of their own. But they're only what they are because God made them and controls them. He's just as much involved in the normal processes of nature as he is when he chooses to bypass them. Usually he respects them and works within them. He thinks they're good. That's why he made them that way in the first place!

In the case of illness, we can fall into the trap of going to the doctor without a thought of God, only turning to him for a 'last resort' miracle if all else fails. But God's Spirit is the source of all kinds of healing. We should call on him first in prayer, and then make our appointment with the doctor.

God usually works through the medical processes he lovingly designed for our good.[2] So we should thank him (as well as the doctor) when the medicine works.

DEEPER HEALING?

Even when the medicine (or the prayer for supernatural healing) 'doesn't work', that's not failure. God's still healing us even if we're left permanently disabled or die.

Paul prayed three times for God to take away a painful physical ailment. But the Lord answered, "My grace is all you need, for my power is greatest when you are weak."[3] In other words, he experienced more of God's love and strength helping him to live with the pain than he would have done in having it removed.

This was true for David Watson too. As he faced the fact that he might die, he put things right in his relationship with God and several other people.[4] He was healed deep in his spirit. He came to see death in a truer perspective and to accept it. He died a more complete person than he had lived.

And for him, as for all Christians, death was the ultimate healing. No more pain, no more frustration, no more sin. A new body in a new world, and Jesus — forever.[5]

Paul, Silas and Timothy gave the church at Thessalonica an approach to prayer which is ideally balanced.

> Be joyful always, pray at all times, be thankful in all circum- stances.[6]

In other words, "Pray about everything, and watch how God answers your prayer. Find what you can thank him for and rejoice in." Then they prayed for the deepest level of healing in the Thessalonians.

> May the God who gives us peace make you holy in every way and keep your whole being — spirit, soul, and body — free from every fault at the coming of our Lord Jesus Christ.[7]

---

1   For one thing, if this became the new norm, it would obviously stop being a miracle, which means something unusual. See 3.6 "Can we really believe in Jesus' miracles?" (page 70).

2   People sometimes say that all the healings in the New Testament were miraculous. Even if this was true, it wouldn't necessarily tell us anything more than that the writers were only recording unusual, eye-catching events. They didn't think it worth taking space to tell us that Paul's wounds from being stoned and flogged healed up in the normal way. But in fact it isn't even true that every New Testament *prescription* is supernatural, let alone every healing. Paul tells Timothy to "take a little

wine … since you are ill so often" (1 Timothy 5:23). Not pray more, or go to someone with a gift of healing, but take something for it.

3   2 Corinthians 12:7-9.

4   He told the story himself in *Fear no Evil* (Hodder and Stoughton, 1984).

5   For more on the Christian view of death, go to 7.1 "What happens when we die?" (page 166).

6   1 Thessalonians 5:16-18.

7   1 Thessalonians 5:23.

4.11 "How can I be sure the Holy Spirit's at work in my church?"[1]

The atmosphere at Church A's Sunday service is almost electric. Everyone looks happy. There's a warm welcome as you arrive. The music lifts the roof off. The preacher's riveting. People give generously in the offering. They stay around for ages afterwards, chatting and laughing.

Church B is a sad contrast. The building's cold and the roof leaks. The organ seems to have got asthma. The sermon struggles to get any attention, let alone reaction. The few people present sit apart from each other and can hardly make themselves heard. They rush to get out at the end.

No prizes for guessing which church most people would say was more filled by the Holy Spirit. In nine cases out of ten they'd probably be right. But not in every case. Although Sunday services are an important shop window, they don't tell us everything that's going on in a church. Churches live and work all week, often out of sight. God sees beyond how things look on the surface; he sees what they're really like underneath.[2]

It's possible Church A is a youth or student church where people know each other well and are on the same wavelength. Perhaps it's in a wealthy neighbourhood; or has a particularly strong, dynamic minister or leadership team. All these things can create a feeling of success.

Church B, on the other hand, may be in a run-down, inner-city area where 70% of the population's Muslim. Or in a remote village, where the minister lives many miles away and can only visit once a fortnight. The few people in Church B may in fact be a bigger, more typical, and more spiritually mature cross-section of their local population than the crowd in Church A.

It's never wise to brand a church 'Spirit-filled' or spiritually dead. Only God can know the true state of heart. And he's almost certainly at work in ways we can't see.

JESUS IN CHARGE

All churches look from one angle like any other human organisation, with human leaders running the show. But the New Testament uses a number of different pictures to show what churches should really be like — a body, a flock, a building, etc. Among other things, these pictures stress that Jesus is the leader in charge. He's the Head on the body; the Shepherd of the flock; the Cornerstone and Capstone of the building.[3]

It's all very well agreeing Jesus *should* be leader of our church. We can probably agree we *want* him to be. But how does it actually happen?

Answer: it's the Holy Spirit's job to make it happen. That's the real sign and test of his presence in our church.

So on Sundays we should be looking for evidence that Jesus is the real host of the meeting, the leader of the service, the person doing the teaching, the name on everyone's lips, mind and heart. Friendly smiles, beautiful music and bright banners are warmly welcome; but they're no substitute.

THE REST OF THE WEEK

The Holy Spirit continues to usher Jesus in as leader of every other church activity throughout the week. He makes what Jesus wants clear to us. Through the Bible, as we read and try to understand it together. Through prayer, as we ask him to guide us. Through the wise ideas and decisions of the church members, especially (but not only) the leaders.

Then he brings us to the point where we agree to follow Jesus' lead together. This is a real toughie! It's desperately difficult to get *ten* human beings to agree on anything, let alone 100 of them. But as the Holy Spirit develops Jesus' character in each of us, he makes it possible for us to unite rather than quarrel.

This doesn't mean you have to give way weakly to other people every time. But the Holy Spirit will at times give you the grace to consent to what others want as a mark of your Christian love. Believe me, that takes real strength to do.

Then as we work together, we need the Holy Spirit's help to make our efforts actually achieve something. Every piece of harmonious teamwork; every person growing more like Jesus; every new person becoming a Christian; every fresh initiative in obedience to the Bible; every advance of God's Kingdom in the world around us — all are signs of the Holy Spirit at work in our church.

None of this would be possible if we were a purely human organisation. Left to ourselves, our churches would grind into the sand and fall apart.

But with the Holy Spirit guiding and enabling us in all these ways, the Church is less an 'organisation' and more a living organism — revived and nourished each day by God himself.

Do your best to preserve the unity which the Spirit gives by means of the peace that binds you together. There is one body and one Spirit ... we must grow up in every way to Christ, who is the head. Under his control all the different parts of the body fit together, and the whole body is held together by every joint with which it is provided. So when each separate part works as it should, the whole body grows and builds itself up through love.[4]

---

1   See also section 6 on THE CHURCH, especially 6.4 "Which Church is the right one?" (page 150).

2   1 Samuel 16:7.

3   Colossians 1:18; John 10:7-16,27-29; 1 Peter

2:4-7. For more about these pictures of the church, go to 6.1 "You can be a Christian without going to church" (page 144).

4   Ephesians 4:3,4,15,16.

4.12 "What's the sin against the Holy Spirit?"

This question is a clear example of why we need to read the Bible carefully, instead of picking up other people's rumours.

Christians down the centuries have heard there's an unforgivable 'sin against the Holy Spirit'. And those with tender consciences immediately wonder if they've committed it.

Let me say at once what it is *not*. It's not masturbation or gay sex, even though ignorant people have sometimes called them unforgivable.[1] Nor is it bad language, evil thoughts, opposing church leaders or playing around with the occult. When we sin in those directions, we can be forgiven if we confess to God.[2]

WHAT THE SIN IS

What Jesus actually said was:

> I assure you that people can be forgiven all their sins and all the evil things they may say. But whoever says evil things against the Holy Spirit will never be forgiven, because he has committed an eternal sin.[3]

Mark the Gospel-writer must have realised people would misunderstand it, because he added an explanation.

> Jesus said this because some people were saying, "He has an evil spirit in him."[4]

The "some people" were in fact Jewish teachers of the law. They had come from Jerusalem specially to inspect Jesus 'exorcising' people, i.e. driving evil spirits out of them.

They couldn't bring themselves to admit that this was God at work. They accused Jesus of having the devil in him. "It is the chief of the demons who gives him the power to drive them out," they said.[5]

"You see what they're doing," says Jesus. "They're calling good bad. They're religious leaders, teachers of God's words. But their attitude has become so anti-God they can't spot him when his actions are staring them in the face. They call him the devil."[6]

Jesus warns that when people are so anti-God that they call his work Satanic, they've reached a point where they can't be forgiven. They've set themselves against God; and the result is, they won't admit they need his forgiveness, or ask for it.

It's not clear on this occasion whether the teachers have finally reached this point. Is Jesus warning them they're in danger? Or is he announcing they've passed the point of no return? Only God can see a person's true state of mind.

So we should never say of anyone that they've committed an unforgivable sin.[7] Yet it may just be right occasionally to warn them they look as if they're heading down that dangerous road. Disobeying God could become such a habit that they end up unable to come back and say sorry.

HOW TO AVOID IT

Two things are very clear, and we should say them to set people's fears at rest.

(1) No-one who worries they may have committed 'the unforgivable sin' has in fact done so. If they'd gone that far, they'd be

past worrying or caring.

(2) No sincere Christian should ever reach this point. If we keep following Jesus each day and stay open to him leading us, there's no way we shall think or call him evil.

The time to worry about ourselves is if or when we catch ourselves doing something we know is wrong in God's sight, but refusing to admit it or stop it. That makes the Holy Spirit sad.[8] He'll give us no peace till we realise what we're doing.

Our part then is to stop stifling him and do whatever he's pressing us to do. When we let him direct and control our lives, there's no danger of sinning against him.[9]

---

1 For more about these, go to 1.5 "Why are Christians so against gay people?" (page 20).
2 See 3.10 "If we're forgiven by God, can we continue to do what's wrong?" (page 79).
3 Mark 3:28,29.
4 Mark 3:30.
5 Mark 3:22.
6 When Jesus talks of the Holy Spirit here, he doesn't mean the later, special sense of the third member of God's three-in-one. He just means God at work in the world.
7 It is not even clear from this incident whether Jesus thinks the sin is repeatable in later generations. He **may** have considered these teachers exceptionally blameworthy because, unlike us, they could see him in action face to face.
8 Ephesians 4:30.
9 Galatians 5:16,25.

1. Think of the three Christians you know best. In one column list the gifts you think each of them has (i.e. what they are good at in serving God). In a second column list which of these qualities the Holy Spirit produces you have seen most clearly in them: love, joy, peace, patience, kindness, goodness, faithfulness, humility, self-control. If possible, tell them what you have written — it will encourage them. And ask them what they would put for you. (Or if that's really impossible, list what you think they would put for you.)

2. What excites you about the Holy Spirit? How can you show him your feelings?

3. How would you answer someone who says, "I think I'm a Christian, but (a) I'm not a very good one, and (b) sometimes I doubt whether it's all true"?

4. How would you answer a Christian who says, "I've tried praying, but it doesn't seem to work"?

5. How would you answer a new Christian who says, "I don't understand the Holy Spirit"?

6. Have you any other questions about the Holy Spirit, not covered in this chapter? Who could you ask?

The Bible is long out of date

How does God 'speak through the Bible'?

What about contradictions?

GOD'S
BOOK

The Bible

5.1 "You can't expect people to read the Bible today. It's boring and out of date and too long!"

BORING?

Yes, *parts* of the Bible will certainly seem boring to people who've never read it before. But I wouldn't recommend people new to the Bible to go near bits like Leviticus or Lamentations for several years.

Start with a Gospel — the story of what Jesus said and did. Go on to the Acts of the Apostles — what Jesus did through his first followers. *These* are not boring! They're telling the most exciting story I've ever come across. God Almighty on a rescue mission to save the human race.

Including me — and you. God died for you. God came back to life for you. God shares life with you. God put it all in a book for you. Boring?!

When the astronauts brought back a lump of moon-rock, people queued for hours just to get a glimpse of it. But in the Bible God's put a great hunk of *heaven*-rock in our hands. God's own words and wisdom in a book we can keep for ever and read any time.

One reason why we often *feel* the Bible's going to be boring is that the devil wants to stop us reading it. It might do us good! So he kids us we've got more interesting and exciting things to do. But what could possibly be more exciting than Almighty God wanting to talk to us?

The devil's the bore — because he's trying to do us out of one of our most valuable possessions as Christians. Now there's one thing to do about an old bore — shut your ears to him ...

OUT OF DATE?

The Bible's certainly *old*. It was probably all written by 100 AD. But not every old book's out of date or replaced by something modern. Chaucer, Shakespeare, Dickens — all wrote before even the 20th century. And every Christmas out come the family pantomimes based on stories older still — Aladdin, Beauty and the Beast, Cinderella.

These writings are called 'timeless'. They don't belong to one age or generation that passes away, to be replaced by a new one. They belong to all time.

How much more so the words of God, giving instructions to the human race. And the actions of God, wrapping himself in the lives of people and nations and churches, to show who he is and what he wants to do with us.

He didn't mean the Bible to be like a newspaper, here today and gone tomorrow. He wants it to last for as long as the world lasts. It's telling us things every human being in every generation needs to know.

God only needed to send his Son to earth to die on the cross once. But the results live on for all time. They belong to you and me 2000 years later as much as they did to Mary and John at the time.

TOO LONG?

Too long for what? No-one's suggesting you try to read the Bible like a thriller in one holiday, or even one plane flight. That's why people broke it down into chapters and verses. They make manageable, reader-friendly episodes to dip into, one at a time.

The Bible's a friend for life. You've got 60 years' worth of God's words in your hands. What did you want? Something the length of a bus ticket?

In any case, you don't have to *read* the Bible, if reading's not your thing. The point of the exercise is not to read though a book. It's to meet God and take in what he wants to say to you. You can **listen** to his words, which is how most people came across them in the first place — the whole Bible's available on tape.[1]

What's more, you don't have to engage with the Bible on your own. Often we hear God best when we come to grips with his word together with other Christians. Sunday services should have at least one Bible reading, and a teaching spot based on it. And all fellowship groups (youth groups, home groups, Christian Unions, etc.) should include time in their programme somewhere for learning from the Bible together.

Psalm 119 is one long prayer to God about his 'Law' — an Old Testament name for its written documents, which made up the Bible as far as it existed at that time. The psalm is full of excitement and praise for such a gift from God, with its commands and promises. Here are some typical verses:

ACCESS ALL AREAS

More important than a good job or college course, even better than close friends and wide interests, the Bible puts God's own words into our hands. It's our access to all-round living (spiritual dimension included). Probably the best 'coming of age' present imaginable.

Some churches or families give Bibles as baptism or confirmation presents. But how about giving another one (a new version) to someone for their 18th birthday? (You could ask for one for yours — or for your *next* birthday if you missed out at 18.)

How can young people keep their lives pure? By obeying your commands.

I delight in following your commands more than in having great wealth.

I study your instructions; I examine your teachings.

I take pleasure in your laws; your commands I will not forget.

The law that you gave means more to me than all the money in the world.

Your word, O LORD, will last for ever; it is eternal in heaven.

How happy I am because of your promises — as happy as someone who finds rich treasure.[2]

1   One source is the Bible Society (www.biblesociety.org.uk). There are also videos showing parts of the Bible being acted out (see p136 under Scripture Union). Much of the Bible is describing historical events; to see them re-enacted may bring us closer to the original impact than just reading about them.

2   Psalm 119:9,14-16,72,89,162.

5.2 "How can the Bible actually help us?"

Only if you open it up and take it in. It's a practical book, the Maker's Manual on how to live. God's our Maker, so he really knows how human life works. Far from being a spoilsport document to rob us of our enjoyment and freedom, his guidebook shows how to get the best out of life. It tells us the only way to live truly free.

For instance, people think God's a killjoy because the Bible says don't have sex outside marriage. But he actually wants to protect the joy of sex. Because he made us, he knows sex is only safe and secure in the lifelong commitment of marriage. Any other relationship runs the danger of misunderstanding and breakdown. That's an atmosphere where sex can't flourish. And that's what the Bible's trying to prevent.[1]

If you try to play a computer game without following the instructions, you're likely to get into a mess. It's the same with the Bible. It'll only help us if we do what it says.

OBEY

Jesus worked out how he should live by obeying God's instructions in the Bible. The devil tempted him to prove he was God's Son by leaping off the top of the Temple without a parachute. But Jesus said no because "the scripture ... says, 'Do not put the Lord your God to the test.'"[2] As far as Jesus was concerned, a commandment in the Bible was God's commandment for him to obey.

Jesus' 'Bible' consisted only of the Old Testament. But he gave his authority to the New Testament in advance.[3] He told his first followers, "Whoever loves me will obey my teaching ... the Holy Spirit ... will ... make you remember all that I have told you"[4]. When they came to write down Jesus' teaching for us, they trusted the Holy Spirit to make sure they got it right.

So when we come across God or Jesus in the Bible telling us to do something, our job is to do it. There was a soldier in the British army called Bill Batt, who became a Christian. Someone gave him a Bible and told him what it was for.

"That's fine", he said. "I'm a soldier. I'm used to obeying orders. Whenever I come across a command in the Bible, I'll put it into practice."

He started reading Matthew's Gospel. He soon came to Jesus' command, "love your enemies"[5]. People usually haggle for hours over what this means. But he simply read on to the next words which tell you how to do it: "pray for those who persecute you".

So he made a list of those fellow-soldiers who were making fun of him since he'd begun reading his Bible and praying in the dormitory at night. He prayed each day for their attitude to change, and for them to become Christians.

One after another, they did. God's instructions work! He gave them to us to help us live life the way he has planned it.

TRUST

So God's instructions in the Bible aren't meant to feel like heavy, oppressive rules. They're more like the instructions on a bottle of medicine. They're there to do us good. They're loving guidance we can trust.

We're bombarded with voices telling us how to live, what to try, what we mustn't miss out on. Adverts promise us the earth. But who do we believe? How do we know they won't con us or let us down? We can trust what God says to be absolutely safe. He loves us totally and wants nothing but the best for us.

When I was reaching the end of my uni course, I had great difficulty in finding a job. I applied for several which sounded really good but didn't get them. Most of my friends got fixed up, but still nothing for me. I felt very down about it and started panicking that I'd never find anything.

I was then asked to lead a Bible study for a school Christian fellowship on Jesus' words in Matthew 6. "So do not start worrying: 'Where will my food come from? or my drink? or my clothes?' ... Your Father in heaven knows that you need all these things. Instead, be concerned above everything else with the Kingdom of God and with what he requires of you, and he will provide you with all these other things."[6] I don't know whether anyone else got anything out of it, but I certainly did! (And I *did* get a job a few weeks later — but I guess that was a bonus. Jesus hadn't exactly promised me a job; but he had told me to trust God for what I really needed instead of worrying about it.)

> The promises of the LORD can be trusted;
> they are as genuine as silver refined seven times in the furnace.[7]
>
> The commands of the LORD are trustworthy,
> giving wisdom to those who lack it.
> The laws of the LORD are right,
> and those who obey them are happy.
> They give knowledge to me, your servant;
> I am rewarded for obeying them.[8]

---

1 See 1.4 "You don't have to get married to live with someone" (page 18).

2 Matthew 4:5-7.

3 For more on what the Old and New Testaments mean, go to 5.7 "Why's the Bible so hard to find your way around?" (page 126).

4 John 14:23,26.

5 Matthew 5:44.

6 Matthew 6:31-33.

7 Psalm 12:6.

8 Psalm 19:7,8,11.

5.3 "How does God 'speak' through the Bible?"

Some Christian teachers talk about God 'speaking' through the Bible. This can be quite a puzzling idea for new Christians.

It doesn't mean a divine voice speaks the words out loud as we look at them. Nor that they sparkle at us with a luminous glow. And definitely not that we should let the Bible's pages fall open at random and then take the first words our eyes see as God's message to us.

It simply means God will teach us and strengthen our faith in him as we get to know his book.

Just occasionally something we read is incredibly relevant to a question or problem we're facing at the moment. One Christian described this as "the Bible punched me on the nose!"

I did a three-year university course and was offered the chance of extending it for a fourth year. As I was asking God whether he wanted me to say yes or no, my daily Bible reading brought me to one of Jesus' parables I didn't remember seeing before. It's about a fig tree which produces no fruit three years running. So the owner decides to cut it down. But the gardener pleads for it, "Leave it alone, sir, just one more year; I will dig round it and put in some manure. Then if the tree bears figs next year, so much the better ... "[1]

I wasn't sure I liked being compared to a fruitless tree. But the parallel to my own question was so striking, I took it as God's answer. I stayed the fourth year, got the qualification, used it in getting my first job — and thanked God for guiding me.

ASKING AND LISTENING

Usually, though, God's simply wanting to show us through the Bible more of the way he thinks and the things he likes. How else can we get to know him?

So it's good to pray before you start reading. Ask him to help you understand this part of his Book. He had it put there in the first place; now he wants to teach you something through it. He's with you as you read or listen.[2]

Then I find it helpful to ask three questions of any passage I read in the Bible.

1. What does it say? This may sound a bit obvious. But some parts are hard to understand. And others have more to them than appears at first reading. They're all worth a careful look. Ask what the writer's getting at.

2. What does God want me to learn from it? It's one thing reading that Jesus said, "Don't worry"[3]. But it's quite another working out how to obey it in daily life. We need to give our lives an overhaul. What sort of things cause us worry? How could God help us put that worry to rest?

This is where Bible reading moves naturally into prayer, and the conversation becomes two-way.

3. Is there something I should do about it over the next 24 hours? Again, it's not enough just to see that God's trying to teach us something. We haven't learnt it — and his words haven't really got through to us — until we do something about it.

So, for example, if you're worried about a friend or member of your family, or your health or work or money, you need to let God get to work on your worry right now. Instead of panicking, ask him to give you peace of mind and help you trust *him* to sort things out. Or if he shows you how to avoid what you're afraid might happen, ask his help to do it straightaway.

That's the sort of way I find God 'speaking' to me through the Bible and getting involved in my life.

HEARING AIDS

There are two big helps which make it much easier for me to hear what God wants to say to me through the Bible.

1. A modern Bible version. Don't use your Granny's olde Englishe black leather presentation copy. Get something in up-to-date language you can understand. The two most popular English translations are the New International Version and the Good News Bible, though there are several more recent ones.[4] Or you might prefer to try Eugene Peterson's *The Message*; it is a rough translation, not word-for-word, but brilliant at expressing the writers' meaning and feelings.[5]

2. Bible-reading notes or tapes. Several publishers produce booklets or audio-cassettes giving a short explanation of a Bible passage for each day, to help you get at what it means and what God's wanting you to learn from it.[6]

Prayers you could pray before reading or listening to a bit of the Bible:

Open my eyes, so that I may see the wonderful truths in your law.[7]

Speak, LORD, your servant is listening.[8]

---

1 Luke 13:6-9.
2 Incidentally, this is why I think people who aren't Christians don't fully understand the Bible. They haven't got the Holy Spirit with them helping them to make sense of it.
3 Matthew 6:34.
4 See 5.9 "Hasn't the Bible been changed?" (page 132) for the difference between them.
5 The whole of the New Testament and four of the Old Testament wisdom books (Job, Psalms, Proverbs and Ecclesiastes), published by NavPress in the USA in 1995, but available in all Christian bookshops in the UK.
6 See page 136 for details.
7 Psalm 119:18.
8 1 Samuel 3:9.

5.4 "Doesn't God speak to us in more direct ways than a book?"

God doesn't speak to us *only* through the Bible. He can tell us a lot about himself through nature — the world all around us, which he made. He can say even more through our conscience — that inner referee which gives us a pretty good idea when we're doing right or wrong. Still more, God can speak to us though our Christian friends — their love and care for us, their wisdom and advice.

But nature, conscience and friends aren't foolproof guides to God's will. They can all get things wrong and give distorted messages.

That's why the Bible is God's *main* way of communicating with us. He made sure it contains everything we need to know; and that it's in a form we can understand.

A written record is more reliable than word of mouth. That's why schools and colleges use books. If the students just relied on going to lessons or lectures, they'd forget half of what was said — and remember the other half wrong!

I keep a diary and photocopies of all my work. I couldn't do without them. People ask me when I did something or what I said, and I've only the dimmest memory. But my computer and filing system bring it all back into play. A document in writing keeps everything in a form we can refer back to at any time. It's a permanent record of what we need to know.

Trying to apply this sort of idea to Christianity is right out of fashion today. How can a relationship with the living God be expressed through printed words on a piece of paper? How can things written at least 2000 years ago still be relevant? And why should what was right then be right now? Everything changes.

GOD

One answer is simply God. He does *not* change.[1] He lives outside time and our changing world. He's put into the Bible his guidelines for how the human race should live. The society we live in keeps changing; but the basic nature and needs of people don't, nor do God's standards and values.

What he's said about us and about himself is binding for all time. He doesn't change his mind or change his tune. When he says something it's the *truth*. And God's truth is so definite and reliable, that one writer called it "true truth" — to distinguish it from the rough half-truths that are the best we can manage.

This is good news. If God says honesty is right and lying is wrong[2], that's what he wants for all time. He has spoken, and his words remain in force. We don't have to fudge everything with hundreds of 'It depends what you mean by's and 'This is only my own personal impression's.[3] He simply requires us, when answering questions or put on oath, to tell the truth, the whole truth and nothing but the truth.

In the same way, if God says Jesus is the only religious leader who can bring God and the human race together, we don't have to agonise for hours about how far Muhammad or Eastern religions put us in touch with God. God has said they don't.[4] If any religion or philosophy or fashionable idea disagrees with the Bible, it must be wrong. But if it agrees with it, then it's right.

God's words in God's book are the standard for us to judge any other idea by. They're the 'fount of all wisdom', where we can find answers to our questions and disagreements.

JESUS

There's a second reason why we need God's words to us in written form. And that is, simply, Jesus. We all long for a truly human, fulfilling life. The only way to achieve it is (a) to follow the teaching and example of Jesus; and (b) to have his own Spirit living in us. But Jesus lived in history, long before we were born. We can't watch him on TV or call him on a phone-in programme. The only way we can *do* (a) and (b) is if we have the written record of Jesus' life and teaching to follow. The pages of the Bible reveal to us the only Jesus there is.

Shortly before he died Moses repeated all God's commands to the Israelites; and he stressed the value of having them written down.

> Remember these commands and cherish them ... Teach them to your children ... *Write them on the doorposts of your houses and on your gates.* Then you and your children will live a long time in the land ...[5]

Just before *he* died Jesus prayed that God's words of truth would keep his followers faithful to him:

> I have made you [God] known to those you gave me out of the world ... I gave them the message that you gave me, and they received it; they know that it is true that I came from you, and they believe that you sent me ... Dedicate them to yourself by means of the truth; your word is truth.[6]

GOD'S LOVE LETTER?

Adrian Plass, Christian humorist and writer, describes the Bible as "a letter to me from God. It starts with 'Dear Adrian' and ends with 'Love, God'. And it's all intended to be there for me — and you of course." *

* From a speech at a Bible Society meeting, reported in the Bible Society newspaper "Word in Action", Issue 73, 1994.

---

1 Malachi 3:6; James 1:17.

2 Ephesians 4:25.

3 Of course, not all statements in the Bible are as clear as this. It may take more time to work out what they mean. See 5.12 "How can ordinary Christians know what it means?" (page 139).

4 1 Timothy 2:5,6. See also 2.10 "Don't all religions worship the same God?" (page 52).

5 Deuteronomy 11:18-21.

6 John 17:6,8,17.

5.5 "Why the Bible rather than any other books?"

All questions about the Bible come back to God. *He* made the Bible different from other books. It is, quite simply, his Book. The Bible says what God wants to say.

He achieved this by getting involved when the Bible was written. He made sure the writers included everything he wanted in it — and nothing he didn't want.

INSPIRED

One way the Bible itself describes this is that God 'inspired' or breathed out the words. Many of the words in the Bible are, of course, the words God himself said. But even those which aren't, he controlled.

This doesn't mean he dictated the whole Bible, page by page, with the human writers as mere shorthand secretaries. Nor does it mean he was a 'spirit guide' putting thoughts into their minds while they tried to listen to him.

They set about their job in the usual way — recording events, giving instruction or composing a song.[1] But he took control of the process and made sure their words expressed his meaning and truth.

The Bible's **both** the words of its human authors **and** the 'word of God'. In much the same way as Jesus is both human and divine.[2]

UNIQUE

This means the Bible is in a different league from all other great books. Some people say Shakespeare, for example, is an 'inspired' writer. They mean something lifts him above the level of writing in weekly magazines. His plays and poems can be incredibly moving. They explore human nature more deeply than perhaps any other writer. They leave you feeling you understand life better.

But Shakespeare remains a human being. He was 'inspired' by his own human mind and spirit. The Bible was inspired by **God**. What it says, God says.

But what about the special books of other religions? The Qur'an for Muslims — or the Bhagavad Gita for Hindus. Didn't God inspire them too?

If he did, then some wires have got crossed somewhere. For the Qur'an says Jesus was just a prophet, not God. And the Bhagavad Gita teaches, among other things, that all people are reincarnated, i.e. they live many lives, one after the other — while the Bible says human beings live on earth only once.[3]

If the Bible's right in saying God inspired it all through, then at the very least the parts of other holy books that disagree with it can't be from God.

So how can we know whether the Bible really is inspired? We can check that the information it gives is reliable.[4] And as time goes by, we can try out its claims and promises about God and find — as I have — that they're reliable too.

But in the last resort, we can only take Jesus' word for it. If we call ourselves Christians, then we believe and obey what Jesus said.

He treated the Bible as God's inspired words. He was 'the Bible man', through and through. He constantly tried to live out the Old Testament prophecies about him.[5] He used the Bible to teach people about himself, and told his followers to do the same.[6]

If Jesus is right, the holy books of other religions aren't the 'word of God'. They contain many uplifting and beautiful thoughts (along with, I must say, a lot of legends and philosophy that become very boring). But they don't lead us to Jesus, so they aren't what God wants to say to the human race, while the Bible is.

ENOUGH

As God's inspired word, the Bible contains everything we need to help us live as Christians.

God can also speak to us through the 'prophetic words' of other people, and through other writings. Such as Christian books that help to explain the Bible, or tell what God's doing in people's lives today. Or the books called the 'Apocrypha' which appear in some Bibles as an extra section.

They're certainly helpful. All Christians who can read will gain something from what others of God's people have written. These books can deepen our faith, our understanding and our love for God. The writers often prayed and asked God to help them write them.

But they don't have the same authority as the Bible does. Nor do those who think they're speaking a word of prophecy. God doesn't say he'll put his words into any other book or speaker in the same way as he did with the Bible.

The Bible remains all we need. We should test every other 'word from God' by it. It'll only be from God if it's true to the teaching and spirit of the Bible.

Peter explains how God controlled the prophecies which make up so much of the Old Testament.

> For no prophetic message ever came just from human will, but people were under the control of the Holy Spirit as they spoke the message that came from God.[7]

In what's almost certainly the last letter he wrote Paul mentions the Holy Spirit only twice, and both refer to the Bible's teaching. The Spirit inspired the Bible (or 'Scripture' as it usually calls itself) to be the Christian teacher's God-given textbook.

> **All Scripture is *inspired by God* and is useful for teaching the truth, rebuking error, correcting faults, and giving instruction for right living ...** [8]

And the Spirit then wants to empower those teachers to stay true to the Bible. Paul tells his young assistant Timothy:

> **Hold firmly to the true words that I taught you, as the example for you to follow ... *Through the power of the Holy Spirit* ... keep the good things that have been entrusted to you.**[9]

---

1   Most of them knew they were serving God as they did so, and probably prayed for his help — but not all of them. Proverbs 31:2-9 for instance, was first spoken by King Lemuel's mother. We have no evidence that she was an Israelite or a worshipper of Israel's God.

2   See 3.3 "Jesus was just a good man" (page 64).

3   See 7.2 "What about reincarnation?" (page 168).

4   See 5.10 "How do we know the Bible's true?" (page 134).

5   E.g. Matthew 26:47-56.

6   Luke 24:27,45-47.

7   2 Peter 1:21.

8   2 Timothy 3:16.

9   2 Timothy 1:13,14.

5.6 "Is it all equally 'inspired'? Shouldn't we read the 'good' bits more than the rest?"

This is a very understandable point of view. Paul's description of love in 1 Corinthians 13, for instance, seems much more uplifting than some of the gory parts of the Old Testament.

GOOD BITS?

But once you go any deeper into the question, it gets very complicated. Who decides which bits are 'good' and 'inspired'? The bits I like may be quite different from the bits you like.

There was a missionary working with a remote and primitive tribe. He painstakingly translated Matthew's Gospel into their language, and told them the story as he finished each part. But he didn't go straight through from chapter 1 to 28. He started with what he thought were the most moving and exciting stories, then gradually filled in Jesus' teaching.

The tribespeople listened politely. But to his dismay they made no move to worship this Jesus who healed people and stilled the storm, then died and came back to life.

He reached the end of the project. He came to the part he'd left till last. It was the long list of Jesus' ancestors in chapter 1. He couldn't see all those Old Testament names meaning anything to them. But he must stay faithful to his task and give them the whole book.

He read them the list, to him the least interesting or stirring part of the Gospel. The impact was electric. They went wild.

"Do you mean all these stories you've been telling us happened to a *real* person? Someone who had parents and grandparents and great-grandparents ... ? This is fantastic! We thought you were telling us legends about a made-up hero."

Different parts of the Bible come alive for different people in different places and at different times.

IFFY BITS?

Some people have wondered how the book of Esther got into the Bible. It doesn't mention the word God even once. But that's because it's telling about a time when God's people were threatened with mass assassination. It was dangerous to talk about God. The book was written partly as an encouragement that God was still looking after his people, even if the powers in the land didn't believe in him and tried to ban him by law.

The book comes back into its own whenever Christians are persecuted.[1] And much the same is true of books like Daniel and Revelation. They may seem a bit far removed from us in the comparatively safe and comfortable West. But they become absolute life-savers when Christians are thrown into prison or put to death for their faith.

Others have turned up their noses at the Song of Songs. It is a string of sexy love poems, talking about love in more fruity terms than you'll find in any magazine problem page. For centuries the Christian Church couldn't believe its eyes, and said the book must 'really' be picture language for the love between — gulp, splutter —God and the Church ... or the Christian soul!

But there's no hint that they were right.[2] Their embarrassment says more about them than about God. I'm *thrilled* God thinks it's worth taking a whole book of the Bible to say that sexual attraction between man and woman is warm, loving, beautiful, fun and important. Have you any objections?!

The Bible records of Jesus' teaching

are only a fraction of all he said. But in them he quotes or refers to 22 of the 39 Old Testament books. He obviously read them all. And from what he said about them, he obviously thought they were all equally God-given and valuable. That's good enough for me.

So I try to get a balanced diet from the whole Bible. The programme I follow to help me read it each day aims to cover the whole New Testament in a three-year cycle and the 'highlights' of the Old Testament every five years.[3]

I will repeat aloud *all* the laws you have given ...

Your commandments are *all* trustworthy ...

And so I follow *all* your instructions ...[4]

1 Jews still read Esther every year, as it explains the origin of their festival Purim.

2 They *were* right that in the Bible human marriage is a picture of the relationship between God and his people (e.g. Hosea; Ephesians 5:22-33). But they were wrong in saying this was the *whole* meaning (or even the *main* meaning) of the Song of Songs.

3 See page 136 for details of these Bible-reading schemes.

4 Psalm 119:13,86,128.

5.7 "Why's the Bible so hard to find your way around?"

Joanne couldn't make it out. She became a Christian last month. And they told her to read the Bible to find out the way God wanted her to live.

So she started at the beginning. She read how God made the world and put the man and woman in the garden. But then it got really weird: murder — bigamy — and an unbelievable family tree where everybody lived for over 500 years.

And never a single instruction for her on how to live as a Christian. Not one! What's it all about?

Many new Christians face this problem — how to make sense of the Bible. It doesn't read like the Highway Code or any other set of instructions we've come across.

In fact it does contain instructions. In books like Proverbs; or the teaching of Jesus in the Gospels, and the apostles in their letters. But how was Joanne to know that?

It takes a long time to learn our way round the Bible. So it makes sense at least in the early days to get some help, and follow a scheme planned by someone who knows more about what's in the Bible and where. There are several good publications with a Bible passage for each day and then a short explanation of it.[1] And there are other books to guide you round the Bible; a Christian bookshop or church bookstall manager could recommend to you what to try.

The reason it's hard to find God's instructions is that he sets them in a much bigger picture. In the Bible he tells the outline story of his relationship with the human race from the beginning of time till the end. And a lot of it's in story form. It gives case studies of people who followed God's instructions — and mostly, people who didn't.

It's in two main parts — the Old Testament and the New Testament. The word 'Testament' (sometimes also called Covenant) is a good clue to what it's about. It means an agreement based on a promise. The Bible's about the two big Promises God gave to a special group of people, who would belong to him and serve him.

OLD TESTAMENT

The first Promise was to a family who grew into a nation, the Israelites. After its first three kings (Saul, David and Solomon), the nation split into two. The northern part kept the name Israel, and the southern part (ruled from Jerusalem by David's descendants) was called Judah. The two kingdoms fell foul of the world powers of their day and went into exile separately — Israel to Assyria in 722 BC, Judah to Babylon in 586 BC. But the Persian empire (which overthrew Babylonia) allowed the people of Judah to return in 539 BC and they became known as Judeans.[2]

The Old Testament has three main sections (see page 128 for full list of contents).

(1) History books, telling the story of God's people from the beginning (Genesis) till their return from exile (Ezra and Nehemiah).

(2) Books of prophecy. These record the messages God gave the people through his spokesmen, the prophets. There are long books with many messages, like Isaiah; and shorter ones with just one story, like Jonah.

(3) In between (1) and (2)[3], there are what came to be called the "Writings", books of poems. The best known are

Psalms, songs and prayers to God or about him; and Proverbs, wise sayings about life, put together by King Solomon and others.

NEW TESTAMENT

The Old Testament prophets foretold how God would send the ultimate, perfect king, to extend his people and throw open a new Promise to the whole world. The New Testament tells how he did it through Jesus. It too has three sections.

(1) The 'Gospels' (meaning Good News) tell the story of Jesus. Acts tells what happened next through his 'apostles' or first followers.

(2) Then come Letters from the apostles to the first churches, encouraging them to keep going as Christians, advising them how to sort out problems and teaching them what they need to know. Most of these letters are from St Paul and members of his team. But there are also letters from Peter, John and James (who was Jesus' brother).

(3) The last book, Revelation, gives a God's eye-view of the spiritual battle in the age we're living in now, after Jesus' return to heaven. It finishes with a glimpse into the future at the end of the world.

A huge range, with great variety, but one main subject: God's dealings with the human race, and his promises to make those who respond into his Special People. You could sum up the whole Bible as — 'God makes and keeps his promises'.

British bank notes carry the words 'I promise to pay the bearer on demand the sum of N pounds'. The Bible is God's promise to give people a completely new life, and then teach them how to live it. No ordinary book!

In one of his letters Paul sums up the heritage God gave to his Old Testament people. The books of the Bible — which he refers to as 'Law' and 'promises' — are right at the centre.

> They are God's people; he made them his children and revealed his glory to them; he made his covenants with them and *gave them the Law*; they have the true worship; *they have received God's promises*; they are descended from the famous Hebrew ancestors; and Christ, as a human being, belongs to their race.[4]

(continued overleaf)

---

1 Details on page 136.

2 After Old Testament times, the name developed into the modern 'Jews'. It is convenient for school RE to call the Old Testament the Jews' holy book, and it is true in one way. But it does not follow that Christians regard it as a less important part of *their* holy book. The New Testament sees itself as the completion of the Old in one integrated whole.

3 This is the order in our English Bibles. In the original Hebrew, the Writings come third after the 'Law' (the name for the first five books of the Bible) and the Prophets (which in their division includes several of the history books as well as the books of prophecy).

4 Romans 9:4,5.

BIBLE AT A GLANCE

OLD TESTAMENT

History	Genesis
	Exodus
	Leviticus
	Numbers
	Deuteronomy
	Joshua
	Judges
	Ruth
	1 and 2 Samuel
	1 and 2 Kings
	1 and 2 Chronicles
	Ezra
	Nehemiah
	Esther
Poetry	Job
	Psalms
	Proverbs
	Ecclesiastes
	Song of Songs
Prophecy	Isaiah
	Jeremiah
	Lamentations
	Ezekiel
	Daniel
	Hosea
	Joel
	Amos
	Obadiah
	Jonah
	Micah
	Nahum
	Habakkuk
	Zephaniah
	Haggai
	Zechariah
	Malachi

NEW TESTAMENT

History		
(Jesus)		Matthew
		Mark
		Luke
		John
(After Jesus' return to heaven)		Acts of the Apostles
Letters		
(Paul and his team to churches)		Romans
		1 and 2 Corinthians
		Galatians
		Ephesians
		Philippians
		Colossians
		1 and 2 Thessalonians
(To individuals)		1 and 2 Timothy
		Titus
		Philemon
(Other writers)		Hebrews
		James
		1 and 2 Peter
		1, 2 and 3 John
		Jude
Prophecy		Revelation

5.8 "Why do people talk about it as one book when there are so many different authors?"

The answer is simply God — and the sort of book he wanted written.

MANY BOOKS

In one sense the Bible's *not* one book; it's 66. The very name Bible means *books*, not book.

It needs to be many books because God wants it to reflect all the ways he speaks to us; all the circumstances we find ourselves in; and all the ways we respond to him.

STORY

Large chunks of the Bible, for example, are a story. Like a TV soap, it's a long-running family saga of what started as one man. Then it follows his descendants and their friends, their enemies, their changes through history.

Although God's the director, he's also the true Father of the family, but with Abraham as his human representative. Near the end of the story God introduces a big plot twist. In the Old days only Abraham's blood descendants could be family members. But then one day God starts adopting children from all countries under the sun.

From Abraham to this bigger, rapidly growing family the story covers about 2000 years. You could, of course, have one writer telling it all at the end of the process. But it's much more lively and interesting to have eyewitnesses writing it down at the time.

So we have Moses and Nehemiah recording their own part of the story; court historians reporting the deeds of the kings of Israel and Judah; some of Jesus' closest followers getting the most important things he did and said written down[1]; and Luke, a member of Paul's mission team, telling how the Church spread round the north of the Mediterranean during its first 30 years.

DIRECT SPEECH

The story shows God at work in the lives of his people. But there are times when he speaks to them more directly, instructing them how to live. This needs a different sort of writer — prophets in the Old Testament when the people or their leaders were often together within earshot; letter-writers in the New Testament when the church fellowships were scattered across different provinces and countries.

But even in the most direct messages from God, he didn't bypass the personalities and abilities of the different speakers and writers. So we have the wounded, sensitive Jeremiah and the blunt, impulsive Jonah; the visions of Ezekiel and the vision-interpreting of Daniel. Their variety reflects the many ways God speaks through human messengers.

In the same way, the New Testament has quite different characters and styles. There's Paul — brittle, brave and brilliant, blazing a trail for Christianity where it had never gone before. But there's also John -deeply loving and reflective, helping younger Christians see through false ideas and stand firm against them.

We need all this variety if we're to get a full grasp of the breadth of God's truth.

POETRY

Another huge chunk of the Bible is in po-etry. But different kinds of poetry, need-ing different kinds of poet, to express the sides of truth that poetry is best for.

There's love, both divine and human — the Psalms sing of the relationship be-

---

1 The fact that there are four Gospels is another example of all this lively variety. The writers give different points of view and build up for us a fuller picture of Jesus.

tween God and his people; the Song of Songs celebrates love between man and woman.

> I love the LORD, because he hears me;
>
> he listens to my prayers.[1]
>
> I hear my lover's voice.
>
> He comes running over the mountains,
>
> racing across the hills to me.[2]

Then there are God's other emotions. Most Old Testament prophecy is in poetry, often expressing God's sorrow or anger.

> "Do you think I enjoy seeing an evil person die?" asks the Sovereign LORD. "No, I would rather see him repent and live."[3]
>
> You [God] marched across the earth in anger;
>
> in fury you trampled the nations.[4]

There's also instruction — Proverbs puts God's wisdom into lively, memorable sound-bites and word-pictures.

> You may make your plans, but God directs your actions.
>
> A nagging wife is like water going drip-drip-drip on a rainy day.[5]

Finally there's deep thinking — Job tackles the problem of suffering and Ecclesiastes the meaning of life.

Job said, "I was born with nothing, and I will die with nothing. The LORD gave, and now he has taken away. May his name be praised!"[6]

> Everything that happens in this world happens at the time God chooses. He sets the time for birth and the time for death ...[7]

ONE BOOK

The Bible's a library of books for all people, for all the stages they pass through and all the moods they feel. Such a vast scope needed and used many writers. There were about 40 of them, spread over different countries and different centuries for about 1500 years.

Yet in spite of all this rich variety, the Bible's really one book after all. It has one main topic: God makes and keeps his promises. One main character: God himself — Father, Son and Holy Spirit. I can only think of one way to explain this extraordinary unity. Behind all the human authors was a divine editor and publisher, planning and co-ordinating what they said. This is why Christians believe the Bible's not just another book; it's God's Book.

1 Psalm 116:1.
2 Song of Songs 2:8.
3 Ezekiel 18:23.
4 Habakkuk 3:12.
5 Proverbs 16:9; 27:15. The original Hebrew is poetry, but the Good News Bible translation is English prose.
6 Job 1:21.
7 Ecclesiastes 3:1,2.

INSIDER GUIDE

to some key Bible words and what they mean

Apostle — The word means someone who is sent - a messenger or missionary. In the New Testament it usually applies to Jesus' 12 closest followers. One of them, Judas Iscariot, betrayed Jesus and then committed suicide. It seems that Jesus called Paul to take his place. Some of these apostles (or people like Mark, Luke and James working very closely with them) wrote the New Testament books. So the New Testament carries the authority of the apostles. And they in turn carry the authority of Jesus. *

Parable — The word means a comparison or illustration. It is usually a story, but sometimes just a word picture. It uses familiar events (such as a wedding, a dinner, finding something after you have lost it) to help us understand spiritual truths (such as what heaven is like or how God feels). Jesus used many parables in his teaching, but there are others in the Bible as well.

Prophet — The word means spokesman, someone who speaks on behalf of someone else. Bible prophets are God's spokesmen or messengers. For long stretches of history the Old Testament prophets were God's main way of telling people what he wanted them to do. Some of them (like Elijah) have only a few messages recorded in the Bible; others (like Isaiah or Jeremiah) have whole books of their prophecies. The word prophet does not in itself mean someone who tells the future, although God's message often did look into the future, just as the Christian Good News does.

Psalm — The word means a song sung to a harp. It refers to any of the songs recorded in the Bible. Most of them come in the Old Testament book of Psalms, which may have been the Temple song-book. But there are other songs (or psalms) throughout the Bible. (Oh, and other instruments were allowed too!) **

---

* Matthew 10:40; John 14:26; 16:12,13; 20:23.
** E.g. Psalm 150:3-5.

5.9 "Hasn't the Bible been changed over the years?"

English translations of the Bible change.

For centuries the English-speaking world was content with the 'Authorised Version' of 1611 (also known as the 'King James Version' after James I who commissioned it).

But in the 20th century there was a flood of new translations to meet the very reasonable desire to have the Bible in modern language. The sheer number of different translations may reflect how fast the language changes now; and the need for Christians to make the faith known to people who don't learn the Bible at school.

MODERN ENGLISH

The two most popular are still the Good News Bible and the New International Version, even though they have been around for over 20 years. They first came out within two years of each other[1], and you may wonder why two different English translations were necessary so close together. Part of the answer is they were aiming for different uses, and so they went for different styles of English.

The NIV set out to be used for reading and preaching in church services. So it aimed to be accurate, clear and recognisable as a descendant of whatever version churches had used before it.

The GNB, on the other hand, broke free from all previous translations. Its goal was to be easily understood by all who speak English as their first language. So it restricted itself to 'common language', a pool of a few thousand words in everyday use.

It also made big use of another technique for easier understanding called 'dynamic equivalence'. This means it doesn't translate the original word-for-word if there's no English expression meaning the same as the Greek or Hebrew. It goes for the English equivalent of the Greek or Hebrew meaning.[2]

So in Psalm 23:5 the NIV follows older translations and puts into English exactly what the Hebrew *says*:

> You anoint my head with oil;
> my cup overflows.

But the GNB recognises that the average reader today needs help in understanding what David *meant* by it. Why should God give me hair oil? And why should it apparently spill into my drink, in excessive quantities?! GNB explains the custom and the mental picture, rather than translating the exact words.

> you welcome me as an honoured guest
> and fill my cup to the brim.

Both are faithful, in their different ways, to what David wrote. And neither changes his meaning.

The arrival of these two translations prompted some earlier ones, such as the New English Bible and the Revised Standard Version, to update themselves. So in the 1990s out came the *Revised English Bible* and the *New* RSV! Not content with this a simplified NIV followed, called 'New Light'. And the GNB revised edition has also been published, although the new Contemporary English Version (CEV) is designed to be a replacement GNB for the year 2000 onwards. Meanwhile a New Century Version, taking the idea of dynamic equivalence even further than GNB, appeared (several years early!) in the form of a Youth Bible.[3]

These revisions followed changes in the English language and 20th century culture. One of them is to use 'inclusive language'. For a long time the English word 'man' translated two different words in the original, one meaning a male human being, the other the whole human race or mankind.

The first edition of GNB translated Psalm 8:3,4:

When I look at the sky, which you have made,
at the moon and the stars, which you set in their places —
what is man, that you think of him;
mere man, that you care for him?

This is no longer acceptable, as it leaves some girls and women feeling ignored or excluded. In the second edition it became:

what are human beings, that you think of them;
mere mortals, that you care for them?

It's a good example of how all the changes are trying to take us *closer* to what the original Bible writers meant, not further away from it.[4]

ORIGINAL ORIGINAL

We no longer possess the actual scroll Isaiah wrote his prophecies on, or Paul his letter to the Romans. But we can be confident we've got very reliable copies.

For one thing, the people who wrote out early copies of the Bible treated God's book as sacred. They thought it a sin to change anything and took great care to make no mistakes.

The result is, the early handwritten copies that have survived have surprisingly few differences between them. And those few are all on minor points. None of them affect any important piece of Christian truth.

What's more, some of those copies are very early indeed compared with other ancient books. Tacitus was a first century Roman historian. The oldest copy we possess of his work was written out 800 years after he first wrote the words. But scholars are quite satisfied it's a reliable copy.

We have complete copies of the four Gospels written little more than 100 years

---

FLESH AND BONES

We need to be warned not to jump to conclusions that the Bible is unreliable the moment we come to a difficulty which we can't answer.

General William Booth, the founder of the Salvation Army, was asked what he did about passages he found hard to understand. He replied: "The same as I do when eating a kipper. I put the bones on the side of my plate and get on with the good meat."

The important thing is to concentrate on the heart of the matter and then come back to the side issues at a later stage.

From Nigel Scotland, *Going by the Book* (Scripture Union, 1991), p.95.

---

after the authors wrote. And we have part of John's Gospel in a copy that may be only 30 or 40 years later than John's own handwritten or dictated work.

You can rest assured: it — and the rest of the Bible — has come down to us with its message unchanged.

It's amazingly reliable. That's one of the reasons why I think God had a hand in putting it all together and looking after it.

---

1 GNB 1976, NIV 1978.
2 All English translations use dynamic equivalence to some extent; otherwise they would sound like a foreigner trying to speak English. But GNB was the first to make it a governing principle. NIV's translators claimed they were treading a middle path between literal and dynamic equivalent translation.
3 1993, Nelson Word.
4 There is a difference here between translations and *paraphrases*, which take the idea of dynamic equivalence so far that, as they themselves admit, they give the modern writer's *impression* of what the Bible means rather than a strict rendering of its words. Examples are J.B. Phillips' version of the New Testament, the Living Bible, and Alan Dale's New World version, widely used in schools. These are excellent for helping people see what the Bible is getting at; but you should not rely on them for an exact translation of what it says.

Good question. Christianity's entirely based on the Bible; and Christians try to guide their daily living by the Bible's instructions. So it's important to know we can rely on it.

The word 'reliable' is probably more helpful than 'true'. The word 'true' is vague; the Bible can be *true* in several different senses.

HISTORY

When people ask if the Bible's *true*, they usually mean, 'Did the events it records really happen?' The historical bits of the Bible tell the story of God's people in two parts: Israel in the Old Testament; the life of Jesus followed by the beginnings of the Church in the New. They claim to be true accounts of events that really happened. Most of these events fit in well with everything else we know about the world at the time. Some are even recorded outside the Bible by other writers of the same time.

The main thing people question about them is that they include miracles. There are many miracles in Jesus' life, but fewer in the rest of the Bible than many people think. They happened mainly in three short historical bursts — during the lives of Moses and Joshua; Elijah and Elisha; and the apostles. These were periods when God was making a new start. If he really is God, he's free to do things how he likes. He's not tied down by the normal processes he has designed for the world.[1]

Remember too that the main point of some stories in the Bible isn't whether they actually happened or not. They're there to teach us something about God, whether the story's fact or fiction. The obvious example is Jesus' parables (his stories like the Good Samaritan or the Lost Son[2]). But it's possible the stories of Job and Jonah in the Old Testament are as much parable as history. Both were real people; and the main outline of their stories is historical. Indeed, it's perfectly possible that every detail happened exactly as recorded (including Job having a second family identical to the first one that died, and God causing a large fish to swallow Jonah and then spew him out)[3].

But neither book comes in the 'historical' section of the Old Testament. And clearly both writers gave the stories a 'moral' or teaching-point — like Jesus' parables, but unlike most Old Testament history books. The punch-line is where God reminds Job that his wisdom is sometimes beyond our understanding; or shames Jonah into understanding that he loves and wants to rescue even Israel's deadly enemies.[4] These would still be true whether the rest of the story's historical or not. With Job losing all his children and all his property on a single day, and the entire population of a city and even the animals wearing sackcloth, both stories have a certain 'Once upon a time' feel to them.[5] They may have been massaged a little to sharpen the teaching-point.

But there are large parts of the Bible that aren't stories at all. In what sense do we expect them to be 'true' or reliable?

PSALMS

Many of them express the writers' feelings towards God. They do so with great openness and honesty. You can find every spiritual feeling there — bad days as well as good. They encourage us to tell God the truth about how we feel — up or down.

But what about the picture they give of God? There's nothing misleading in it provided we remember the Psalms are written in poetic and pictorial language.

This will help us when we read words like:

Smoke poured out of his nostrils,

a consuming flame and burning coals from his mouth.

He tore the sky apart and came down

with a dark cloud under his feet.[6]

This doesn't mean David (the writer) thought God was a cosmic dragon breathing out flames, or an alien from another universe dive-bombing down to earth. But he knew that God has strong feelings, anger included. And he had an experience that made him sure of the fact that God does step in decisively and take action for us when we're in need.

PROPHECY

The heart of prophecy is a human speaker saying exactly what God wants to say. But how do we know whether their claim to speak God's words is true?

Moses gave God's Old Testament people a test to help them know.

You may wonder how you can tell when a prophet's message does not come from the LORD. If a prophet speaks in the name of the LORD and what he says does not come true, then it is not the LORD's message.[7]

The prophets often warned how God would punish the people if they carried on doing wrong. And sure enough, God's judgment fell time and again. Israel's enemies invaded and finally took the people into exile. This showed they were true prophets, speaking God's words.

But they also made a long-range forecast that one day a perfect King would come to set the people free. They foretold aspects of Jesus' life with extraordinary detail. His special position as God's Son.[8] His birth to a virgin mother.[9] His place of birth.[10] His blameless life.[11] His death by crucifixion.[12] His death achieving forgiveness for our sins.[13] His return to life after death.[14] And his return to heaven at God's right-hand side.[15]

Those prophets' words also came true. So we may be sure we can have complete confidence in the books they wrote.

1   For more about miracles go to 3.6 "Can we really believe in Jesus' miracles?" (page 70). For more about the rest of Jesus' life go to 3.2 "Are the records of Jesus' life really true?" (page 62). One other part of the Bible people question is its story of how the world began. For more on that go to 2.3 "Hasn't evolution disproved God?" (page 38).

2   Luke 10:25-37; 15:11-32.

3   Job 1:2,18,19; 42:13; Jonah 1:17; 2:10.

4   Job 38:1-42:6; Jonah 4:11.

5   Job 1:13-18; Jonah 3:8.

6   Psalm 18:8,9.

7   Deuteronomy 18:21,22.

8   Psalm 2:7 (Matthew 3:17); Hosea 11:1 (Matthew 2:15).

9   Isaiah 7:14 (Matthew 1:22,23).

10 Micah 5:2 (Matthew 2:5,6).

11 Isaiah 53:7,9 (1 Peter 2:22,23).

12 Psalm 22:1,7,8,16,18 (Matthew 27:35,39,43,46).

13 Isaiah 53:5,6 (1 Peter 2:24,25).

14 Psalm 16:10 (Acts 2:31).

15 Psalm 110:1 (Acts 2:33-35).

NOTES TO HELP YOU READ THE BIBLE

SCRIPTURE UNION

Bread for the Journey

Very flexible Bible reading notes. They can be read in a group as well as by an individual; they can be read straight through or dipped into. They are bitesize looks at the Bible making you think about your identity, your relationship with the Christian community, who Jesus is and what your relationship with him can be. These would perhaps be good for a brand new Christian.

Disclosure

A very youth oriented look at the Christian life. Interviews and articles about Christian musicians interspersed with close-up looks at many Bible passages and Christian issues ranging from relationships with non-Christians to who is Jesus? This gives you a huge number of topics looked at in a brief but relevant way.

Scripture Union, 207-209 Queensway, Bletchley, Milton Keynes MK2 2EB.

Tel: 01908 856000. Fax: 01908 856004.

Email: info@scriptureunion.org.uk Website: www.scriptureunion.org.uk

THE BIBLE READING FELLOWSHIP

New Daylight

A daily Bible reading complete with helpful comments and a prayer for the day. A fresh and regular look at many different passages from the Bible. Geared towards more knowledgeable Christians.

Bible Reading Fellowship, First Floor, Elsfield Hall, 15-17 Elsfield Way, Oxford OX2 8FG.

Tel: 01865 319700. Email: enquiries@brf.org.uk Website: www.brf.org.uk

CRUSADE FOR WORLD REVIVAL

Every Day with Jesus

This very popular series is a daily Bible reading tool which offers: practical help with life's challenges; insights into the deeper truths of Scripture; and six in-depth topics each year. Every Day with Jesus is also available through email where a new reading will be delivered to you every day.

CWR, Freepost, PO Box 230, Farnham, Surrey GU9 8BR.

Tel: 01252 784710. Website: www.cwr.org.uk

5.11 "Aren't there any mistakes? What about the contradictions?"

Gods Book

It all depends what you mean by mistake or contradiction — and Bible![1]

There have certainly been mistakes in some *printings* or *translations* of the Bible. But those were not mistakes in the Bible books themselves. And later versions have put them right.

In 1631 King Charles I's printers in London put out a thousand copies of the Bible with a small but fatal mistake. They left the word 'not' out of the seventh commandment. So it read "Thou *shalt* commit adultery". The red-faced printers had to withdraw it mighty fast!

The Church of England Prayer Book includes a version of the Psalms dating from 1539 and still used in a few places today. In Psalm 105:18 it describes Joseph in prison: "the iron entered into his soul". It sounds a marvellous phrase for depression and has become an English saying to mean that. Unfortunately it's a mistake — the Hebrew means 'his *soul* (or whole life) entered into the *iron* (or chains of prison)'. Good News Bible translates much more reliably, "an iron collar was round his neck".

MISTAKES?

Most things which have been accused of being mistakes turn out later to be misunderstandings. Further research or discoveries show them not to be mistakes at all.

John's Gospel tells of Jesus healing a paralysed man at a pool with five porches called Bethzatha.[2] For a long time scholars accused John of making the story up, because no-one had found any pool with five porches in the ruins of Jerusalem. "It's a typical John-like picture story," they said. "He just means that the Old Testament law with its first five books in the Bible leaves people morally paralysed and unable to get into the water of forgiveness and new life."

But then in 1888 an archaeological dig discovered the base of the five porches around the remains of a pool. It's one of the best sites for pilgrims to Jerusalem today.

This teaches us to be humble when we come across what look like mistakes or contradictions. If we can't explain them ourselves, we should ask someone else. If they can't explain them either, we should pray and wait. The fact that we haven't yet found an answer doesn't mean there isn't one.

CONTRADICTIONS?

We don't need to be afraid of contradictions in the Bible. Some new Christians fear that if a friend of theirs can point out a place where the Bible contradicts itself, that disproves the whole of Christianity.

It's an unnecessary over-reaction. Some people who aren't Christians may like to kid themselves they can think that way; it may suit their point of view to imagine that Christianity is a load of rubbish. But no Christian need be so naive.

We certainly shouldn't dismiss the whole Bible because we've found one or two seeming contradictions in it. We are in touch with the living God. The Bible stores his words and actions for us. As he's totally powerful and totally wise, it's hardly

---

1 Some people think the Bible must be wrong about how the world began. 'Science' or 'evolution' has disproved it, they say. But how far has the theory of evolution been proved? And how literally did the author of Genesis 1 mean us to take his story of creation? There is a fuller discussion of these questions in 2.3 "Hasn't evolution disproved God?" on page 38.

2 John 5:1-8.

surprising that parts of his book are hard to take in all at once. It includes truths that are in tension with each other. They stretch our minds and make us wrestle. This is good for us; it deepens our trust in God.

Take one example. Jesus taught us to pray, "Lead us not into temptation"[1]. But Paul appears to say that God *does* allow us to be tempted or tested.

> Every test that you have experienced is the kind that normally comes to people. But God keeps his promise, and he will not allow you to be tested beyond your power to remain firm; at the time you are put to the test, he will give you the strength to endure it,
> and so provide you with a way out.[2]

I'm not sure how to resolve the seeming difference between these two statements.

Good News Bible translates the Lord's Prayer, "Do not bring us to *hard* testing". I.e. we ask God to keep the promise Paul mentions, and protect us from any testing that's too hard for us. That may well be right; I'm not quite certain.

But I don't let it worry me or put me off the Bible. I don't let it stop me praying the Lord's Prayer. And it doesn't for one moment make me question Paul's words which I've found to be true. God *has* helped me to endure or escape testing, time after time after time.

---

1 Matthew 6:13, New International Version and older translations.
2 1 Corinthians 10:13.

5.12 "Different churches and experts understand the Bible in different ways. So how can ordinary Christians know what it means?"

When I became a Christian, I was full of excitement over what I was reading in the Bible. So much so that I enthusiastically shared my discoveries with a minister connected with our youth group. His reaction left me reeling. Instead of offering encouragement, he poured cold water on my ideas by always saying, "Ah, but there are other interpretations of this passage". So I've great sympathy with this question.

But the confusion this leaves us feeling as ordinary Christians can easily seem much worse than it should. God doesn't mean the Bible to be impossible to understand. And he definitely doesn't think it's all just a matter of opinion.

SIMPLE RULES

In fact there are very few parts of the Bible Christians disagree about. And even with those, you can usually work out the best understanding if you follow these simple rules.

1. Ask the Holy Spirit to help you understand. He looked after the Bible as the writers wrote it. Now he wants to guide you as you read it.

2. Don't decide the answer *before* you look at the Bible. Come to it with an open mind, and let God convince you through it.

3. Try to work out what the original writer or speaker meant.

4. Look carefully at the surrounding words, as they will often help you see what your passage means.

5. Check that your understanding doesn't clash with another part of the Bible. If it does, you must have got it wrong.

6. When the Old and New Testaments appear to disagree, follow the New. It has fulfilled and in some ways replaced the Old.[1]

A SIMPLE EXAMPLE

Talking about the Holy Spirit, Jesus said "he will lead you into all the truth"[2].

Some people have picked up these words and claimed the Holy Spirit is guiding all scientific and medical research, and even all philosophical discussion about the meaning of life. After all, they say, they're all part of "all the truth" about God's world.

But a closer look at what Jesus said shows that's not what he was talking about. The full sentence these words come from says,

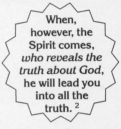

When, however, the Spirit comes, *who reveals the truth about God*, he will lead you into all the truth. [2]

So he's not talking about life in general, but the truth about God.

"Ah!" say some other people, "the Holy Spirit reveals truth about God. So he is at work in all religions. They all believe in God."

But again, that's not what Jesus meant. As the word "however" at the beginning of the sentence shows, it doesn't make full sense on its own. We need to read the one before.

(continued overleaf)

---

1 The most obvious example is animal sacrifices. God commanded his Old Testament people to offer these as part of their worship. The New Testament explains that they were a foretaste of Jesus' perfect sacrifice of himself on the cross; now that it is complete, animal sacrifices are no longer needed (Hebrews 10:1-17).

2 John 16:13.

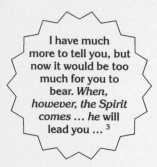

I have much more to tell you, but now it would be too much for you to bear. *When, however, the Spirit comes ... he will lead you ...* [3]

So the truth the Spirit teaches is continuing the truth Jesus taught. He reveals the truth of the **Christian** faith.

This is where a third group of people pounce. "We're Christians," they say, "but God is showing us new truths no previous Christians have seen. The Spirit is leading us into **all** the truth. Up till now Christians have only known **some** of the truth." [4]

Wrong again! They're assuming that when Jesus says the Spirit will lead **you** into all the truth, he means **us** — 21st century Christians.

But he clearly doesn't. The 'you' in the second sentence must be the same as the 'you' in the one before.

I have much more to tell *you*, but *now* it would be too much for *you* to bear. [3]

Obviously he means the people he was talking to at the time — the apostles who were with him on the night before he died.

They couldn't take in any more of what Jesus needed to teach them. They were too confused and worried and tired at that stage. But later, when the Spirit came on the Day of Pentecost, he would fill in the gaps. Then they could preach and teach the truth about Jesus and help the Church to grow.

The record in the New Testament of what they taught makes the Holy Spirit's teaching available to all later generations of Christians.

That's why Christian Churches have always believed the whole Christian faith is contained in the Bible. No new idea is Christian if the Bible disagrees with it.

There's no suggestion that 21st century Christians will discover new parts of the Christian faith which the apostles knew nothing about!

What's more, that disputed verse is not a confusing saying which no-one can understand for certain. It's really quite clear.[5]

The explanation of your teachings gives light and brings wisdom to the ignorant.[6]

---

3   John 16:12-13.

4   This can sound particularly appealing to people who want to be told *exactly* what to believe, rather than think things through themselves.

5   In fairness I should admit there are still *some* parts of the Bible which are not 100% clear. For an example, go to 6.5 "Why's the Church so divided, e.g. over the ordination of women?" (page 153), or 7.9 "Won't there be signs that it's nearly the end of the world?" (page 182). When we can't see how to sort out different understandings, we should take the approach recommended in 5.11 "Aren't there any mistakes?" (page 137).

6   Psalm 119:130.

SO WHAT?

1. How would you answer someone who says, "The Ten Commandments are out of date" (you will find the Ten Commandments in Exodus 20)?
2. How helpful do you find your present way of 'listening' to the Bible and praying? How might you be able to make it more helpful?
3. Think back over the last week. What do you think God has said to you — or been trying to say to you? Through what channel? What do you think he was trying to say to you through the last piece of the Bible you read or thought about? What should you do about it now?
4. What is your favourite bit of the Bible at the moment? How would you explain to a new Christian what it means to you?
5. Think of any bit of the Bible which has seemed to you to be a mistake or contradiction, or just hard to understand. See if you can make more sense of it now, with the help of the suggestions in 5.11 and/or 5.12.
6. Use the approach from 5.12 to work out exactly what you think Jesus meant by John 14:26. What do you think he wants us to do about it now?

You can be a Christian without going to church

Why is church so boring?

Why does the church spend so much money on buildings when people are starving?

6

GOD's
PEOPLE
The Church

6.1 "You can be a Christian without going to church."

Well, yeeeeeeeeeees. (To pronounce this word right, you need gritted teeth and quite a lot of aggro.) I suppose there's a speck of truth in that.

Obviously if you were the only survivor of an air crash on a desert island, you'd still be a Christian. But there'd be no-one to join you for Family Praise on Sunday morning.

In normal conditions, though, God doesn't mean you to be a Christian on your own. If you try, half of your Christian discipleship will be a pale shadow of what it should be; the other half won't happen at all. That's why God made the Church.

YOU BELONG

The trouble with the 'you don't have to go to church' idea is, it completely misunderstands what the Church is for. The Church doesn't exist to 'go to'. This wrong idea has come about from people confusing the **Church** with the building where church members meet. And perhaps with the meetings that go on in it.

But the Church isn't bricks and mortar. It's people. The Greek word for 'church' in the New Testament means 'assembly' or 'group of people specially called together'. All Christians belong automatically to Jesus' Church from the moment they start following him, because he has specially called them to be his people.

The New Testament uses a number of word pictures to describe the Church. One is Jesus' **body**, in which we're all different limbs — eyes, ears, hands, feet, etc. Another is Jesus' **family** where we're all sisters and brothers. A third is his **flock**, with us as the sheep. Yet another's a **vine** where we're the branches.[1]

The left ear doesn't 'go to' the body; it's part of it. A daughter isn't only in the family for an hour on Sundays; she's a lifelong member. A lamb doesn't subscribe to the flock magazine; it belongs. A branch can't say, "I think I'll visit another vine this week"; it's inextricably entwined.

I admit the New Testament also pictures the Church as a building.[2] But it's only a picture. It's **not** meant to allow us to call a real building a church! The picture is making this same important point. Each brick's a vital part of the whole. Take just one away and the whole building's in danger of collapse.

God makes us members of his Church for us to play an active part in it. If one foot or child or lamb or branch is missing, the whole thing's weakened and damaged.

SO JOIN

We need to join a local church[3] and get stuck in. We all have something to contribute. If that's not easy to arrange straightaway, see the church leaders and offer to help in any way you can. Tell them what experience you've had and what you think you're some good at.

Don't worry if they ask you to do very humble tasks at first. Someone's got to do them. Why not you? Don't be too proud; develop the attitude of being ready to serve.

And of course you will want to be part of at least one gathering of the church family each Sunday. Or if you don't **want** to, you **need** to. How else will you get to know these sisters and brothers you belong to?

Let us be concerned for one another, to help one another to show love and to do good. Let us not give up the habit of meeting together, as some are doing. Instead, let us encourage one another all the more, since you see that the Day of the Lord is coming nearer.[4]

---

1 Body — 1 Corinthians 12:12-27. Family — Mark 3:31-35. Flock — John 10:7-16,27-29. Vine — John 15:1-8,16.

2 Ephesians 2:20-22; 1 Peter 2:4,5.

3 Or it may be some other Christian group using a name like 'fellowship', 'assembly' or 'family centre' rather than the actual word church.

4 Hebrews 10:24,25.

I suspect 95% of Christians would tell you we go to church to worship God.

But I think they're wrong.

Not that God doesn't want us to worship him! He designed us to find our deepest fulfilment and enjoyment as human beings in loving and serving him.

But the New Testament makes a big change to how and when and where we should worship. And surprisingly few Christians seem to have noticed it.

WORSHIP?

In the Old Testament God agreed to meet his people in his holy place — first the 'tabernacle' or tent of meeting, later the temple. There they were to worship him. God's Old Testament people did indeed go to their equivalent of church to worship God. But in the New Testament *we* are the temple![1] God is with us wherever we are. *That's* where we should worship him.

When Jesus was asked about worship, he made a quite revolutionary statement:

> ... a time is coming when you will worship the Father neither on this mountain nor in Jerusalem ... a time is coming and has now come when the true worshippers will worship the Father in spirit and truth, for they are the kind of worshippers the Father seeks.[2]

It's so important, Jesus repeats himself for emphasis.

> God is spirit, and his worshippers must worship in spirit and in truth.[2]

In the New Testament, we don't worship in Jerusalem or 'in church', but "in spirit and in truth". Not in a 'worship area' or 'worship centre', but in the *depth* of our being ('spirit') and with the *whole* of our being ('truth'). Worship's no longer just an outward activity; it's something our whole lives express because of who we are. It's a living, intimate relationship with God as our Father.

Paul takes this up, almost as a direct quote, in his carefully worded letter to the Romans. When he turns to how we should live as Christians, his very opening words are:

> Offer yourselves as a living sacrifice to God, dedicated to his service and pleasing to him. *This is the true worship that you should offer.* Do not conform yourselves to the standards of this world, but let God transform you inwardly by a complete change of your mind.[3]

God's New Testament people don't give him dead animals in worship. We give him ourselves as a *living* sacrifice. We put everything we have and are into his hands to direct and control. This is a non-stop, lifelong, day-in day-out process from the moment we start as Christians till we die. We let God gradually and continuously transform our minds. As we learn to think his way, so we begin to live his way.

So worship's not just on Sundays; it's our whole life. It's not just when we're with other Christians; it's whatever company we're in, including when we're alone. It's not just the 'religious bit' of singing and praying; it's work, play, rest, food, sleep and all. Worship's the whole slant of our life — belonging to God, dedicated to his service and pleasing to him.

The commonest Old Testament Hebrew word for 'worship' means to bow down in surrender. The commonest New Testament Greek word means to kiss as a sign of homage. When we say we worship Jesus, we mean he's Lord of everything we do, say and think.

It's quite misleading to say, 'I worship at such and such Church'. It abuses both words — worship and church — by locking them up in a building. There's no set time or place for worship. You should worship wherever you are — all the time! Going to church to worship would be like going to hospital to breathe!

CHURCH?

So why bother going?

The New Testament's equally clear on this. It never uses the word 'worship' to describe what Christians do when they meet. Naturally they'll praise God and pray to him together because that's the way their lives are pointed towards him the whole time.

Equally naturally we often find we praise and pray better when we're together. This is because we help each other focus on God, come clean with him and tell him all that's on our hearts. Surrounded by the rest of God's people, we're more aware of him, more open to what he wants to say to us and give us, more able to pour out our love for him in return.

The whole point of meeting *together* is to build each other up in this way, and in countless others. We go to church to *work*. Through our different gifts — teaching, encouraging, caring, serving, leading, giving, making music or making merry, whatever they may be — we strengthen each other to trust Jesus and serve him till we next meet.[4]

We're quite wrong to call them 'worship services'. Better names would be, simply, 'meetings' or 'assemblies'; or 'Christians together', or 'Family Festival' or 'Bodybuilding Workout'; or even *'Training* for Worship'.

We don't *go to* church to worship God. We should *leave* our cosy church fellowship equipped to worship God throughout the coming week.

This means the so-called 'coffee and chat after the service' is just as much the reason why we meet as the hymns and prayers and sermon before it. It's sometimes our best chance to build each other up — to talk about our joys and sorrows, needs and problems, and above all about Jesus. What a shame when people scurry off home unfed.

> When you come together, everyone has a hymn, or a word of instruction, a revelation, a tongue or an interpretation. *All of these must be done for the strengthening of the church.*[5]

> Let the word of Christ dwell in you richly *as you teach and admonish one another with all wisdom,* and as you sing psalms, hymns and spiritual songs with gratitude in your hearts to God.[6]

1 1 Corinthians 3:16; 6:19,20; Ephesians 2:20-22. See 4.6 "What's the Holy Spirit trying to do to me?" (page 96).

2 John 4:21,23,24 New International Version.

3 Romans 12:1,2.

4 This is what the 'gifts of the Spirit' are for. For more on what they are, go to 4.9 "What are the 'gifts' of the Holy Spirit?" (page 103).

5 1 Corinthians 14:26 New International Version.

6 Colossians 3:16 New International Version.

6.3 "Why is church so boring? It's full of old people, hypocrites and people with problems."

In a world of fast-moving fashion, the Church's image is rarely cutting edge. Many churches have been shamefully slow to listen to their younger members or give them space and encouragement to use their own gifts and ideas.

But this isn't the whole picture.[1]

BORING?

The Christian Church certainly wasn't boring when it began.

> Many miracles and wonders were being done through the apostles, and everyone was filled with awe. All the believers continued together in close fellowship and shared their belongings with one another. Day after day they met as a group in the Temple, and they had their meals together in their homes, eating with glad and humble hearts, praising God, and enjoying the good will of all the people. And every day the Lord added to their group those who were being saved.[2]

And in spite of horrific persecution, the Church kept on growing. It's still here today.

So what went wrong? Well, to be fair, there's still a lot right about the Church. There's a huge amount of encouraging Christian work among young people. But because it's good news, it doesn't get reported.

But to be equally fair, there's also a shameful lot wrong with the Church. The biggest problem is simply — *us*. Churches are imperfect because they are made up of human beings. Most other organisations are equally disappointing, because they have this alarmingly high proportion of *people* inside them.

Of course, it's very easy to knock *any* organisation when you stand on the sidelines and see all the faults. Think how the press treat the England football and cricket teams!

If that's how you're treating your church, then its second biggest problem is — *you*. You're damaging it still further by not joining in. Jesus doesn't mean you to have that luxury.

When you started as a Christian he made you a member of his Church or body. And the only way to make that real is to belong to one particular local church or Christian group. And belonging means joining in its activities and playing your part in them.[3]

When you do, there will be a sudden change. There'll be something a bit more worthwhile for your age-group to do, because you are there. It'll be that little bit less boring. Nothing startling at first, perhaps; but at least it's a start.

HYPOCRITES?

As you take an active part in your church, you'll get to know some of the other members. And here's my word of prophecy: you'll find they're not all such hypocrites as you thought.

Outsiders *think* Christians are hypocrites, pretending to be better people than we are. But if we're real Christians we *know* we're wrongdoers through and through. We only look happy because Jesus has taken the punishment for all that wrong off our shoulders. And now he's slowly but surely making us better than we were. But no credit to us. All the good work is his.

OLD PEOPLE?

Some churches don't have all that many older members; it may be because of the area they're in or the style of their services and activities. But most churches have more *old* adults than *young* adults; many have more old people than average for the country's population. At first sight it looks very worrying for the Church's future. But in fact it's a good sign.

It's nothing to do with Christianity only appealing to past generations. It shows it really lasts the course. If churches had nothing but young people, *that* would be worrying. It would mean that when people became that bit more mature, they lost their faith. They would have found that Jesus had nothing to say to people facing the problems of middle or old age.

But quite the reverse. As people become older Jesus becomes steadily more real to them. Unlike Hollywood or fashion companies, God isn't only interested in us while we're young, fit and beautiful.

Older people have a wealth of experience to offer those of us who are younger. In heaven I reckon you will find out that many of them were among your greatest supporters. You will discover how much faith they had in you and how they prayed for you every day.

PROBLEM PEOPLE?

OK, so there are plenty of these in churches too. But where else should they be? Who else will care for them and try to help? After all, Jesus said he came to befriend the problem people. I'd be really worried if they couldn't find him among us.

But who am I to talk about them and us? I'm not exactly problem-free myself. And I've a shrewd suspicion you're not either. Isn't that why we need Jesus in the first place?

Jesus described his followers like this:

> People who are well do not need a doctor, but only those who are sick. I have not come to call respectable people, but outcasts.[4]

He's not very impressed with people who do nothing but moan and criticise. *They're* the real hypocrites!

> How dare you say to your brother, 'Please, let me take that speck out of your eye,' when you have a log in your own eye? You hypocrite! First take the log out of your own eye, and then you will be able to see clearly to take the speck out of your brother's eye.[5]

His agenda for the Church is incredibly challenging — but hardly boring.

> You are like salt for the whole human race. But if salt loses its saltiness, there is no way to make it salty again. It has become worthless, so it is thrown out and people trample on it.
>
> You are like light for the whole world ... your light must shine before people, so that they will see the good things you do and praise your Father in heaven.[6]

---

1 See also 4.11 "How can I be sure the Holy Spirit's at work in my church?" (page 108).

2 Acts 2:43,44,46,47.

3 See also 6.1 "You can be a Christian without going to church" (page 144).

4 Mark 2:17.

5 Matthew 7:4,5.

6 Matthew 5:13,14,16.

6.4 "Why are there so many Churches, all believing different things but claiming to be right? Which Church is the right one?"

The Gospels record Jesus using the word 'church' just twice.

Once he means the sum total of all his followers in every country and every century.[1] People sometimes call this the 'universal' Church. I give this meaning of the word a capital C to show the difference from the other meaning Jesus gave it.

This was the local gathering of believers who meet together.[2]

The rest of the New Testament never uses the word in any other sense than the local church or the universal Church.

So presumably Jesus never meant Christians to club together in different subgroups calling themselves the *Church* of England, the Methodist *Church*, the *Church* of Rome, etc. To try to avoid confusion, I call these 'denominations' rather than churches.

One summer I crawled in a traffic jam along the main street of a seaside resort. We passed the church buildings of six different denominations. Here we are telling people Jesus can cure all the hate and fighting in the world. We claim he makes us love each other. But our own house is so badly divided, no-one will believe us.

It's a symptom of illness which needs to be healed.

MAJOR SPLITS

It's easy enough to say we should get back together. It's a great deal harder to do. Many good brains worked on it for most of the 20th century. They had pockets of success where denominations have reunited or agreed to work towards it.[3] And rather more hopeful is when all the Christians on a new housing estate, say, work together and share a building.

But the difficulties are enormous because they're buried so deep in history.

Once a split has occurred, people tend to polarise on one side or the other. They magnify the differences to make their own position feel stronger. And it becomes desperately hard to heal the rift.

There are two major splits in worldwide Christianity. The first happened in the 11th and 12th centuries. The chief political vehicle which enabled Christianity to grow and spread during its first 1000 years was the Roman empire. Because of this the church in Rome gradually came to take on a leading role over the other churches.

But the areas to the east resisted this development and asserted their independence of Rome. This was a gradual process, accelerated when the empire itself crumbled into two halves. Its eastern and stronger capital was Constantinople (modern Istanbul in Turkey). The churches based on it have come down to us today as the 'Eastern Orthodox' churches, most notably in Greece and Russia.

The churches in the west, on the other hand, accepted Rome's lead. We know them today as the Roman Catholic churches under the leadership of the Pope.

The differences between them may not seem vast; they are more about style than belief. At heart they still boil down to who should be in charge.

The second split happened in the 16th and 17th centuries among the western churches. There were a number of reform movements protesting at various corruptions in the Roman system. They met strong resistance and so broke off to form new churches. They were never one coherent movement, so the result was a number of different denominations, conveniently grouped under the one label Protestant.

In setting up 'reformed' churches, the Protestants weren't starting something completely new. They were trying to re-form the original pattern on the lines of the New Testament. It was a reaction against what they saw as Rome allowing ideas not clearly taught in the Bible (such as the authority of the Pope) to have equal authority alongside the Bible.

In this attempt I believe they were right. Of course, as human beings, they made many mistakes. In an imperfect world we shall never reach agreement on *everything* in the Bible. But Jesus taught his followers to take the Bible as the place where they could find the broad lines of God's will laid down.[4] And it seems to me it must be the starting-place for any attempt to reach agreement and unity today.

MINOR SPLITS

The Protestant churches have always officially accepted the Bible's overall authority. (Sadly there have been many leaders and teachers who have disputed it, but this has not altered the official position of any of the denominations). So the differences between them are comparatively small. Most of them are to do with how we organise church life.

On top of that, some offer baptism to the babies of Christian parents, while others (such as Baptists) hold that baptism should only be for people old enough to believe for themselves. And several groups of churches (often given the umbrella title of Pentecostals) have pioneered the reappearance of some spiritual gifts which seemed almost to have died out, such as the ability to speak in a language you've never learnt or bring instantaneous healing.[5] The 'charismatic movement' has helped to spread these and other emphases across all the denominations.

Most are agreed these aren't major differences. They happily accept each other as Christians.

NEW CHURCHES?

There are some who seem to have given up altogether on the older denominations. They're often called 'New Churches'.[6] They've reacted in despair at the lack of spirituality in traditional churches. I often feel this frustration myself — almost to the point of being overwhelmed. But I'm not convinced it's right to break away and form another new group, which'll simply become yet another denomination. Baptists, Methodists, Salvation Army and all — they were once 'New Churches' themselves.

It seems to me far better to stay within a church and pray for it (and me!) to grow more spiritual, united rather than divided. There's no one 'right' denomination. All are trying to follow Jesus and serve him in their different ways.

But not all local churches seem equally

good to me at teaching and obeying the

1 Matthew 16:18.   2 Matthew 18:17.

3 The 'United Reformed Church' is one example in Britain (most Presbyterian and Congregational churches joined to form it). There are other examples in other countries.

4 Matthew 5:17-20. See also 5.2 "How can the Bible actually help us?" (page 116), and 6.9 "What's heresy?" (page 161).

5 For more on this, go to 4.9 "What are the 'gifts' of the Spirit?" (page 103).

6 To begin with, they were known as 'House Churches', because they met in people's houses or other 'non-church' buildings. But many of them are now very large and well established, and have built buildings of their own! See also 6.7 "Why does the Church spend so much money on buildings?" (page 157).

Bible. If this is where Jesus said we find God's will, it has to be top priority. Many of the splits in history have happened because one side or other haven't made the Bible their top priority.

So my advice to anyone wondering which church to join is this. Forget the denomination or label — that doesn't matter. But check that they try at every meeting to work out what God's saying to them through the Bible. If they do, their heart's in the right place. Join them.

One of Jesus' last prayers on earth was for his followers to enjoy the spiritual unity he shares with his Father.

I pray that they all may be one. Father! May they be in us, just as you are in me and I am in you. May they be one, so that the world will believe that you sent me.[7]

6

GOD'S PEOPLE

7   John 17:21.

6.5 "Why's the Church so divided, e.g. over the ordination of women? And why has the Church got such a bad record on the treatment of women?"

Let's take the second question first. It's a sad fact that Christians over the centuries have been slow to understand the Bible and obey it. Too often we've copied the world around us without seeing that Jesus wanted us to be different.

WOMEN IN GENERAL

Treating women as second-class citizens is a glaring example. Nothing could be clearer than Paul's wonderful charter of equality:

> ... there is no difference between Jews and Gentiles, between slaves and free people, *between men and women;* you are all one in union with Christ Jesus.[1]

But the Church in England took 1800 years to see the logical consequence of this for slaves — they should be set free!

We've taken even longer to allow women their full birthright in church life. They're equal human beings with men in God's sight. They're equal Christians, equal members of God's family, equal partners in being the body of Christ on earth.

It's easy to blame past generations of Christians for their failures. But we should be humble enough to realise we're probably guilty of equally shameful blind spots. We should ask God to show us what they are and help us put them right.

WOMEN IN LEADERSHIP

Back to the first question. The reason why Christians disagree over the 'ordination' of women (i.e. appointing women to lead and preach in churches) is, there appears to be a clash in the New Testament's teaching. And we don't yet agree on how to resolve it.

For the same Paul who wrote the charter of equality also says:

> As in all the churches of God's people, the women should keep quiet in the meetings. They are not allowed to speak; as the Jewish law says, they must not be in charge.[2]
>
> Women should learn in silence and all humility. I do not allow them to teach or to have authority over men; they must keep quiet.[3]

We must take note of this. Christians should follow Jesus in yielding to the Bible's authority. We can't simply ignore parts of it because they're unfashionable.

Paul certainly appears to say women shouldn't be in charge or teach in church. For many Christians that settles the matter. The ordination of women must be wrong. They argue that Paul's 'women's charter' talks about their equal standing before God; but his 'no leading or teaching' instructions talk about their function in church meetings.

Others (including me) are unconvinced because it doesn't explain *why* people of equal standing should have these *unequal* functions. Also, when you put them back in the chapters they come from, both passages take on a quite different emphasis.[4]

The first passage comes from 1 Corinthians 14. In that chapter Paul asks

1 Galatians 3:28.
2 1 Corinthians 14:33,34.
3 1 Timothy 2:11,12.
4 Looking at a passage's surroundings is a vital clue to understanding it. See 5.12 "Different churches and experts understand the Bible in different ways" (page 139).

various groups (tongues speakers, prophets, and now women) to keep quiet if they're being disruptive. All should give way to the need for the meeting as a whole to be in harmony and peace.[5] But that doesn't mean they should **never** speak.[6]

The second passage comes from 1 Timothy 2.[7] Here the word translated 'have authority' means 'be a dictator'. Paul's not objecting to women doing **any** teaching, but doing so in an over-authoritarian way.

So despite first appearances I don't think these two passages rule women out from leading and teaching in churches alongside men.

But I wouldn't myself want them ordained. I can't see that the New Testament includes anything equivalent to modern church ordination. There's no suggestion that a church should have one overall leader — apart from Jesus! New Testament churches had leadership teams of elders.[8] They were commissioned with prayer and hands laid on their heads, but they didn't then become a separate caste of 'clergy' or 'priests'. Ordination creates a sad split between clergy and 'lay' people, right against the spirit of Paul's cry, "you are all one in Christ". Rather than ordain women, I want to **un**ordain men!

But I accept that not all Christians agree with me in these understandings of the Bible. We're still at the stage of needing to do more praying, thinking, reading and listening to each other.

For the time being we're not agreed. But that doesn't mean we need be **disagreeable** to each other — or separated from each other.

It can't be beyond Jesus' people to find ways to differ in peace. And — the point where we started — to find ways to let Christian women develop their ministry in church life.

---

5   1 Corinthians 14:26-33,40.

6   Indeed, only three chapters earlier (1 Corinthians 11:5) Paul clearly expects women to take part in public prayer and prophecy.

7   This is one of the few chapters in the New Testament that really is difficult to understand. There are several different interpretations.

8   Acts 14:23; Philippians 1:1; Titus 1:5.

6.6 "What's the connection between the Church and other Christian groups people belong to?"

There's a host of these other Christian groups.

Some are gatherings of Christians in their work-place — school, college, factory or office Christian Unions. Some are specialist activities for one age-group, especially youth — Youth for Christ, for example, or Scripture Union holidays. Others support Christian mission going on somewhere else — prayer groups, fund-raising events and so on.

NOT A CHURCH ...

They're not part of a local church, but have their own leaders and organisers.

Nor are they themselves in the usual sense of the word *a church*. They don't gather all the Christians in the local community. Often they're a narrow cross-section of people, linked by age or special interest. They don't offer a full range of church activities. Usually they don't feel it right to provide baptism themselves; and sometimes not the Lord's Supper either.[1]

Yet they're a gathering of Christians. When they pray and study the Bible, work together and care for each other, it's hard to say how they're less 'church' than any other collection of Christ's people.

They may not be a local church or even part of one; but they are part of the worldwide Church.[2] They're a genuine expression of Christ's Body, although they're not a complete body as a church is.

Some people have tried to define these groups more precisely. They've coined the word 'parachurch'! The Greek word 'para' can mean next to or alongside. These groups aren't themselves churches; but they're alongside the churches, giving invaluable help and extending what they can do. They concentrate on specialist tasks which many local churches would be unable to do alone.

... BUT A COLONY

Here's another way of looking at them. The commonest theme of Jesus' teaching —especially in the first three Gospels — is 'the kingdom of God'. By this he means not a country (like the *United* Kingdom), but any person, any group, any activity where God's in control. This kingdom will only come fully into its own in the next life. But already, in this world, Jesus the King has invaded and set up colonies where his kingdom has come and his will is done.[3]

This idea of the Kingdom goes wider than the Church. The Kingdom is wherever Jesus is bringing justice, peace and wholeness in the world; the Church is the family of his people. Clearly these smaller, more specialist groups are part of the Kingdom, in a way that they're not so obviously part of a church. They're not a body; but they're an arm or leg of Christ's advancing kingdom. They're building up God's people; living out God's standards; radiating God's love to people in need; signs of hope in a world that often runs out of hope.

Every Christian needs to belong actively to a local church. Many Christians will do themselves and others a power of good by being part of one of these 'kingdom groups' as well. I did most of my early Christian learning and growing

---

1 For more about baptism and the Lord's Supper, see 6.8 "What are baptism and communion all about?" (page 159).

2 See 6.4 "Why are there so many Churches?" (page 150).

3 See also 2.12 "What does God do all the time?" (page 56).

in a university Christian Union and helping to run school holiday parties.

Here's to the growing invasion — in every community, work-place, college and school in your country!

The prophet Isaiah foresaw the growth of Jesus' kingdom.

His royal power
will continue to grow;
his kingdom will always be at peace.
He will rule as King David's successor,
basing his power on right and justice,
from now until the end of time.
The LORD Almighty is
determined to do all
this.[4]

Jesus promises his presence and power to all his kingdom groups, however small.

... whenever two of you on earth agree about anything you pray for, it will be done for you by my Father in heaven. For where two or three come together in my name, I am there with them.[5]

---

4   Isaiah 9:7.
5   Matthew 18:19,20.

6.7 "Why does the Church spend so much money on buildings when people are starving in the Third World?"

'Church' means people. People who need to meet together. And in most climates (certainly in the UK) that means meeting indoors.

BUILDINGS

To meet indoors you have three options:

1. Use a member's home if it's big enough.

2. Hire a hall belonging to someone else.

3. Buy or build your own meeting house.

The early Christian churches had to use Option 1 before they became respectable and rich enough to have their own buildings. Many churches use it today for their smaller 'home groups'.

You'll find Option 2 here and there. Many of the 'new churches' (who don't belong to the traditional groupings like C of E, Baptist, Methodist, etc.) started this way. Some other churches have a phase of meeting in someone else's building if they outgrow their own and it needs extending or other major repairs. And groups of churches often hire a larger building for a joint mission or celebration meeting.

But the vast majority use Option 3. Many of them didn't actually choose it in living memory. It's literally come with the territory — an inherited church building passed on from previous generations and still in use — often despite serious problems. Large old buildings are expensive to heat, maintain and insure. Open prayer, drama and dance, small discussion groups, etc. are next to impossible with pillars and pews.

Obviously it's convenient to own your own building. You can leave furniture, books, screens, musical instruments, etc. where you want them. And once you've got rid of an old building, it would be desperately expensive to change your mind later and buy another piece of land in as good a place.

It's fine if churches put their building to good use on weekdays as well as Sundays, and for a major part of each day. But can churches who use their building for only a few hours each week really justify the vast amount of money they sink into it? Some are good at finding ways for the local community to use it through the week. But often this is the church hall rather than the Sunday meeting space.

PEOPLE

Is it right for Christian groups to spend up to half their money on owning a building when they could give most of it more directly to people? Those starving in the Third World have a big claim on us, certainly. But so do other people in need. Churches in poorer countries haven't a fraction of the resources we have here; we should find a way of sharing.

And what about homeless people in our own country? Including, perhaps, Christians who feel they belong or need to work in more expensive areas, but can't afford to live there. If churches want to invest in buildings, perhaps the first priority should be homes for missionaries and ministers. Or helping young people with starter mortgages.

A second priority should surely be to bring the Good News to people who aren't yet Christians. A building to help us do that is more important than a building for us to hold private meetings in. Many churches find outsiders are put off a traditional 'church building'. But a shop, coffee bar or advice centre offer more neutral ground where people can receive welcome and friendship.

(continued overleaf)

God calls his people to be only temporary residents on earth. Our real home's in heaven. He wants us to sit loose to material possessions. Many churches forced to do without a building for a while find a glorious freedom to experiment and concentrate on what's really important.

So shouldn't our churches have the courage to borrow the buildings we need? Or at least consider it seriously rather than assume we should automatically own them? There may not be a lot we can do about this at once; but let's be ready to face the possibility when the chance comes in future.

Peter taught Christians the right attitude to life on earth.

> I appeal to you, my friends, as strangers and refugees in this world![1]

Jesus taught us, in the same way, to sit loose to wealth and security.

> Do not store up riches for yourselves here on earth, where moths and rust destroy, and robbers break in and steal. Instead, store up riches for yourselves in heaven ...[2]

Paul and Timothy saw this attitude in the churches of Philippi, Thessalonica and Berea towards the famine-stricken Christians in Jerusalem.

> ... even though they are very poor ... they gave as much as they could, and even more than they could. Of their own free will they begged us and pleaded for the privilege of having a part in helping God's people in Judea.[3]

6 GOD'S PEOPLE

---

1   1 Peter 2:11.
2   Matthew 6:19,20.
3   2 Corinthians 8:2-4.

6.8 "What are baptism and communion all about? How important are they?"

Jesus told us to do them. If we're Christians we must obey him. That's how important they are.

COMMANDS

Almost his last command before he died was, "Do this [eat bread and drink wine] in memory of me"[1]. Almost his last command before he returned to heaven was:

> Go, then, to all peoples everywhere and make them my disciples: *baptize them in the name of the Father, the Son, and the Holy Spirit,* and teach them to obey everything I have commanded you.[2]

So if you're a disciple of Jesus, you should be baptised. If you haven't been, ask the leaders of your church to arrange it.

If you were baptised as a baby but received no Christian upbringing, ask their advice whether you should be baptised again. Ideally it shouldn't be necessary; by leading you to become a Christian, God has fulfilled his baptism promises to you. But some feel that baptism of babies is never valid because there are no recorded cases in the New Testament. In fairness we must say the New Testament doesn't give clear directions about this, so there should be no hard and fast rules.

In the same way, if you're a disciple of Jesus, you should be sharing regularly in the Lord's Supper. (Different churches call this memorial meal 'Breaking of Bread', 'Holy Communion', 'Eucharist' or 'Mass', each emphasising different parts of the service.[3]) Most churches welcome 'all who love Jesus' to their communion services.

But if your church require you to become a member or be confirmed first, ask to talk it over with the leaders.

But why are baptism and communion so important? What are they all about?

SACRAMENTS

They're technically known as 'sacraments'. This means they're dramatised pictures of what God does for us inwardly and spiritually.

Baptism's a picture of how we start as Christians.[4] Some churches submerge you in water, others just sprinkle you. Submerging (usually called total immersion) is probably what happened in New Testament times. But the intention's the same, and both forms express part of the sacrament's meaning.

The 'old' you — the person you were on your own before you started following Jesus — needed drastic treatment. You needed to be washed clean from all your wrongdoing — that's the picture in sprinkling. But as your wrongdoing disqualified you from entering heaven, you also needed to die, be buried and start life all over again — that's the picture in immersion.

Because Jesus died in your place, God's able to forgive you and give you new life. So he fills you and floods you with his Spirit. As you emerge from under the water, you're demonstrating the truth that

---

1 1 Corinthians 11:24,25.

2 Matthew 28:19,20.

3 'Communion' means sharing, with God and with each other. 'Eucharist' means thanksgiving. 'Mass' (the Roman Catholic name for the service) is the least central; it comes from the Latin word at the very end of the service, meaning "you are *dismissed*"!

4 See also 4.8 "What do people mean by being 'renewed in the Spirit'?" (page 100).

God has made you a new person, spiritually alive. Some churches offer you a new name at this point to show clearly what's happened.

The Lord's Supper is a picture of living as Christians from our baptism onwards. We need strength to keep going and to live up to Jesus' standards; so he 'feeds' us himself with his own Spirit. We continue to sin; so he goes on and on making real to us the forgiveness he achieved for us when his body was broken and his blood spilt. We share life with him now and for all eternity; so we eat with him a foretaste of the banquet he's preparing for us in heaven.[5]

The simple meal combines all these ideas in an incredibly powerful way. The table pictures Jesus' dinner table. The bread pictures the spiritual life and nourishment we receive from Jesus who called himself "living bread from heaven."[6]

The wine pictures Jesus cleansing us from our sins because he died in our place.

But these sacraments or 'picture services' aren't *just* pictures. The water of baptism, the bread and wine of the Supper are God's promises made visible. As we respond to his promises with love and trust, God fulfils them. He actually does for us inwardly and spiritually what the pictures show outwardly and physically.

As we go through the water, turning our back on our old ways and putting our trust in Jesus, we're forgiven and filled with his Spirit. As we open our empty hands for the bread and wine, we're forgiven and fed with his life.

In this way the sacraments are exactly parallel to the Bible. Just as it feeds us spiritually, so do they. They're simply a different channel. *It's* God's word written and read; *they're* God's word acted out.

5   Matthew 26:27-29.
6   John 6:51.

6.9 "What's heresy? How would I know if it was necessary to leave a church?"

Heresy means false teaching. Ideas which are untrue to the teaching of the Bible as a whole, and especially the New Testament.

It's been common from the earliest days of the Church. Most of the New Testament letters are fighting against it in one form or another.

> False prophets appeared in the past among the people, and in the same way false teachers will appear among you. They will bring in destructive, untrue doctrines ['heresies' — NIV], and will deny the Master who redeemed them, and so they will bring upon themselves sudden destruction.[1]

"Denying the Master" probably means saying that what he taught isn't true or doesn't matter.

The New Testament contains examples of this false teaching which are still around today. One is that Jesus is not fully divine in the sense of God come to earth as a human being.[2]

Another is to encourage a loose sexual lifestyle. Jesus reinforced and even strengthened the Old Testament's high view of marriage as the only relationship where God allows sex.[3] But Christian teachers have always been under pressure to relax the rules a bit.

LEAVING THE BIBLE

The heresy underlying all other heresies is simply to teach that the Bible doesn't have God's authority. Once you lose that measuring stick of what's Christian and what isn't, you can teach what you like. And who can say you're wrong?

The result the New Testament seems to fear most is that the Good News itself gets changed. You can't teach Paul much about strong language. But did even he ever say anything stronger than this double-barrelled blast?

> ... even if we or an angel from heaven should preach to you a gospel that is different from the one we preached to you, may he be condemned to hell! We have said it before, and now I say it again: if anyone preaches to you a gospel that is different from the one you accepted, may he be condemned to hell![4]

On another occasion Paul helpfully summarises the Good News which he and his team preached.

> I want to remind you, my brothers and sisters, of the Good News which I preached to you ... that Christ died for our sins, as written in the Scriptures; that he was buried and that he was raised to life three days later, as written in the Scriptures; that he appeared to Peter and then to all twelve apostles ...[5]

I suggest this should be the basic test we apply in choosing a church to join.[6] Do they proclaim the Good News of Jesus dying for our sins, but now alive again as Lord of our lives? And do they teach the

---

1 E.g. 1 John 4:2,3. For more on Jesus being divine, go to 3.3 "Jesus was just a good man" (page 64).

2 Mark 10:7-9. See 1.4 "You don't have to get married to live with someone" (page 18).

3 Galatians 1:8,9.

4 2 Peter 2:1.

5 1 Cor. 15:1,3-5.

6 See 6.4 "Which Church is the right one?" (page 150).

GOD'S PEOPLE — SO WHAT?

Bible as the way to meet Jesus and learn about him today?

LEAVING A CHURCH

Tragically we may have to use the same test if ever we face the need to leave a church. It's not something we should do for trivial reasons (e.g. changing to St Vitus' up the road because they've got a new Sacred Dance group). It brings great pain all round, and isn't something God wants to happen.

But if the leadership of a church make quite clear — after questioning, discussion and prayer — that they've no intention of preaching the Good News and teaching the Bible, it may be the only course open to us.

The New Testament usually assumes that someone in authority will stop the rot. False teachers should be challenged and removed from their position of influence.[7] The Holy Spirit's able to keep hold of those who want to stay true to the faith.[8]

But in Revelation 3 Jesus has to speak directly through John to the church in Sardis, who seem to have gone pretty thoroughly off the rails:

> I know what you are doing; I know that you have the reputation of being alive, even though you are dead! So wake up, and strengthen what you still have before it dies completely ... Remember...what you were taught and what you heard; obey it and turn from your sins. If you do not wake up, I will come upon you like a thief, and you will not even know the time when I will come.[9]

Jesus pleads with erring churches to return to his teaching. But there comes a time when even he gives them up.

1. How would you explain that church membership is more than just 'going to church on Sundays' to a friend or member of your family who is not a Christian and thinks you're becoming a religious maniac?
2. In what ways are you serving Jesus in (a) your church fellowship; (b) any other Christian group you belong to? How do you think he might want your service to become more effective?
3. What is one thing you find difficult at the moment in being a Christian? How might your church or smaller fellowship group help you with it?
4. What do you like best and least about your church fellowship? How might you be able to do something positive about your chief dislike, without upsetting other people?
5. In what ways could your church or other Christian groups you belong to helpfully work together with another similar group? Pick one of your ideas and plan how you could actually start making it happen.
6. What seems to you most valuable about the Communion service? How could you make more of it?

---

7 E.g. 1 Timothy 1:3,19,20; 5:19,20.
8 2 Timothy 1:11-14.
9 Revelation 3:1-3.

ISSUING DENIALS

Some groups who call themselves Christian, but who
"deny the Master" — Jesus himself.

Christian Science

"Jesus is not the Christ."
"If there had never existed such a
person as the Galilean Prophet, it
would make no difference to me."
"His disciples believed Jesus to be
dead, while he was in the
sepulchre, whereas he was alive." *

Spiritualism

"Jesus Christ was not divine. He is
now an advanced spirit in the sixth
sphere. He never claimed to be
God manifest in the flesh and does
not at present."
"The miraculous conception of
Christ is merely a fabulous tale."
"Spiritualism sees in the death of
Jesus an illustration of the martyr
spirit, of that unselfish and heroic
devotion to humanity which ever
characterised the life of Jesus, but
no special atoning value in his
sufferings and death." **

Jehovah's Witnesses

"When Jesus was on earth, he was
a perfect man, nothing more and
nothing less."
"Jesus was not God the Son."
"Christ Jesus the divine was born
three days after the Crucifixion."
***

Mormons (Church of Jesus Christ of Latter-day Saints)

"When the Virgin Mary conceived
the child Jesus, the Father had
begotten him in his own likeness.
He was not begotten of the Holy
Ghost. And who is the Father? He is
the first of the human family ... "
"If the Son was begotten by the
Holy Ghost, it would be very
dangerous to baptise and confirm
females and give the Holy Ghost to
them, lest he should beget children
to be palmed upon the Elders of the
people, bringing the Elders into
great difficulties."
"We say it was Jesus Christ who was
married (at Cana) to the Marys and
Martha, whereby he could see his
seed before he was crucified." ****

* Mary Baker Eddy, *Miscellaneous
Writings*, p.84; *The First Church of
Christ, Scientist, and Miscellany*,
pp.318,319; *Science and Health with
Key to the Scriptures*, 44:28-9.

** Dr Weisse, *Demonology or
Spiritualism*, p.141; *Spiritualism*,
p.141; *The A.B.C. of Spiritualism*,
Q.19.

*** J.F. Rutherford, *Reconciliation*, p.111;
p.113; *Deliverance*, p.245.

**** Brigham Young, *Journal of
Discourses*, Vol. I, p.50; p.51; Orson
Hyde, *Journal*, Vol. II, p.80.

7

GOD'S PLANS

The Future

All the human eye sees is the collapse of the body. The machine stops; the battery's run out.

Many people think they're no more than a body and a mind. So death must be the end. The person simply ceases to exist.

Jesus insists that death isn't the end. According to him, the 'soul' or real person lives on.[1] Our deepest feelings echo this. It's hard to believe that so much experience and wisdom, so much creativity and sensitivity just disappear.

But Jesus goes further.

FAR BETTER

Life after death, according to Jesus, isn't meant just to continue things as we have known them. He wants it to be the gateway to something far better.[2]

He spoke of eternal life as something Christians begin as soon as we put our trust in him.[3] But the party really gets going after we die and get rid of everything that goes wrong and holds us back on earth.[4]

Jesus did more than just teach this. He showed what he meant by returning to life after death himself. He saw himself as the trail-blazer — the first of many millions who would move on to a fuller life when they died. He told his Father as he prayed for his followers, "I want them to be with me where I am, so that they may see my glory"[5].

BODY AND SOUL

The apostle Paul went on to make clear that we won't be bodiless spirits floating round in space. We shall have new bodies in a new world after death. But they'll be new, better, perfect bodies to fit a new, better, perfect earth.[6]

> When the body is buried, it is mortal; when raised, it will be immortal. When buried, it is ugly and weak; when raised, it will be beautiful and strong. When buried, it is a physical body; when raised, it will be a spiritual body.[7]

Some people wonder whether this means we should be buried rather than cremated. How can our body be raised like Jesus' if it's been burnt?

We needn't worry. There may be other reasons which make us prefer to be buried or cremated. But cremation will not spoil our prospects after death. After all, God will be dealing with people who died in fires, bomb explosions and air crashes. He'll take the 'seed' of the person we were and grow us into the full flower of the person we have it in us to become.

WHEN WE DIE — OR WHEN THE WORLD ENDS?

When exactly shall we experience all of this? There seems on the face of it to be a clash between different parts of the New Testament.

Jesus told the criminal who died on the cross beside him, "*today* you will be in Paradise with me"[8]. That sounds as if we can expect to be in heaven with Jesus as soon as we die.

But Paul makes it sound as if we shall only come alive again when Jesus comes back to earth at the end of the world. "Those who have died believing in Christ will rise to life first; then we who are living at that time will be gathered up along with them".[9]

I suspect the difference is more

imaginary than real. I think it arises because it's impossible for our human minds to understand how things will happen when we leave the world of time and enter eternity. We can only think in terms of time, with one thing happening after another: death first, then receiving our 'resurrection bodies' later when Jesus returns to earth. In the dimension of eternity, though, we shall probably experience it all at once.

On the one hand, I guess the first thing we're aware of when we die will be Jesus; this is what he promised the convict who died with him. But on the other, we shall find the new world is complete — full of the Christians who were still alive on earth when we died.

Listen to this secret truth: ... when the last trumpet sounds, we shall all be changed in an instant, as quickly as the blinking of an eye ... the dead will be raised, never to die again ... For what is mortal must be changed into what is immortal; what will die must be changed into what cannot die. So when this takes place, and the mortal has been changed into the immortal, then the scripture will come true: "Death is destroyed; victory is complete!"[10]

1   E.g. John 11:25,26. For more on the human soul, go to 1.2 "Human beings are just an advanced kind of machine or animal" (page 14).

2   Luke 16:20-22.

3   John 5:24.

4   Matthew 8:11; 26:29; 6:19,20.

5   John 17:24.

6   For more about the new earth, see 7.3 "What will heaven be like?" (page 170).

7   1 Corinthians 15:42-44.

8   Luke 23:43. Many Christians believe on the strength of this that we go to heaven when we die, and stay there until Jesus comes back to bring the world to an end. This is a perfectly possible understanding of the New Testament. But others take the view that I spell out in the rest of this answer.

9   1 Thessalonians 4:16,17. Paul also refers to those who have already died as being 'asleep' (1 Corinthians 15:20); this may be simply a poetic description of how they appear to us, or it may imply an unconscious wait till Jesus comes back to earth. For more on Jesus' return to earth, go to 7.8 "Will Jesus really come back?" (page 180).

10   1 Corinthians 15:51-54.

WE BELIEVE ...

We look for the resurrection of the dead,
and the life of the world to come.

— From the Nicene Creed

REFLECTION

I used to think —
Loving life so greatly —
That to die would be
Like leaving a party
Before the end.

Now I know that the party
Is really happening
Somewhere else;
That the light and the music —
Escaping in snatches
To make the pulse beat
And the tempo quicken —
Come from a long way
Away.

And I know too
That when I get there
The music will never
End.

Evangeline Paterson

7 GOD'S PLANS

7.2 "What about reincarnation and that feeling you've been somewhere before?"

You may have had that feeling. You're visiting somewhere new — on holiday abroad, perhaps, or a famous house open to the public. You're about to go round a corner. And suddenly you *know* what you'll see next. A split second later the view comes in sight — and you were right!

Or you're listening to two people talking. Suddenly you know exactly what they're going to say next. And sure enough, they do.

These experiences leave you wondering, "Have I been here before?" Often there's no way you could have been. So the idea crops up: "Perhaps I visited this place — or heard this conversation — in a previous life."

REINCARNATION

This ties in with the idea of reincarnation. It comes from the Eastern religions of Hinduism and Buddhism. It became fashionable in the West in the 1960s and has since taken on a new lease of life with the growth of Eastern-influenced New Age teachings. It got a fresh burst of publicity in 1998, when the former England football manager Glen Hoddle announced his belief in it in an interview that cost him his job.

'Reincarnation' means entering another body to live on earth for a second or further time. Hinduism and Buddhism teach that the soul of each person does this many times, perhaps hundreds.

The law of 'karma' decides what sort of body or circumstances we'll have next time round. If we're good in this life, we go up the scale in the next. If we're bad, we go down.

CYCLE OR ROAD?

Reincarnation fits the Eastern view of life as an almost endless series of cycles. Life goes round and round. The same things happen over and over again. The eventual aim is to progress one day to perfection.

You'll then at last be set free from the ceaseless round of existence. You'll no longer be condemned to be a separate being. You'll be absorbed into the unconscious peace of nothingness.

This is very different from the religion of the Bible. If the Eastern view of life is like a perpetually revolving wheel, the Bible (and Muslim) view's like travelling along a road. You start at a point called birth. You journey through life. Finally you reach your journey's end called death. You then move on to the next life, still as a separate being called you.

> Seventy years is all we have — eighty years, if we are strong ... life is soon over, and we are gone.[1]
>
> Everyone must die once, and after that be judged by God.[2]

What happens to each one of us will also happen to the whole world. It's not going to spin in space forever. God has great plans for it. There'll be a new heaven and earth.[3]

The Bible never mentions reincarnation. Some people think resurrection and reincarnation are the same thing. But they're not. Reincarnation is living again on this earth in another body. Resurrection is having our own body 'translated' or 'reformatted' on to the new earth.[4]

So how do we explain that feeling of 'I've been here before'? Perhaps the scientists are right when they suggest a sort of delayed consciousness — especially when we're tired or daydreaming, and the two halves of our brain don't synchronise. The event actually happens a fraction of a second before our waking senses take it in. But our subconscious is that fraction of a second ahead. It feeds the information to our mind slightly faster than our eyes and ears. And so we seem to know already what they're going to see and hear.

It's less romantic than the idea of a previous existence. But from a Bible viewpoint, it seems more likely to be the truth.

---

1   Psalm 90:10.

2   Hebrews 9:27.

3   Revelation 21:1. For more on this, go to 7.3
    "What will heaven be like?" (page 170).

4   1 Corinthians 15:42-44,53,54. See also 7.1
    "What happens when we die?" (page 166).

7.3 "What will heaven be like?"

Quite *unlike* most of what we've been led to suppose.[1]

The Bible doesn't teach that we'll spend eternity in some misty, floaty place above the bright blue sky. In fact, it doesn't say we'll be in heaven at all! Heaven is where God is now; but in the future he and we are going to be somewhere else.

There are glimpses of this future all through the Bible. But the fullest sight we get is at the end of Revelation. John gets a sneak preview of what lies in store, and is allowed to pass it on to us.

Because it's a vision or dream, some of it's in a sort of picture code. But we can get the general message clearly enough.

> Then I saw a new heaven and a new earth. The first heaven and the first earth disappeared, and the sea vanished.[2]

Our future isn't in some vague heaven which we find hard to imagine, but on a new earth where we shall naturally feel at home. But it will have no sea. This isn't to stop us swimming (I expect there will be plenty of rivers and swimming pools!). It's because on our present, first earth, the sea separates us into different continents and countries. On the new earth all races and nations will unite under one King.

> I saw the Holy City, the new Jerusalem, coming down out of heaven from God, prepared and ready ...[3]

We shall all live in the perfect city, designed and constructed by God. But not in heaven; it comes down *from* heaven, ready-made for the new earth.

> I heard a loud voice speaking from the throne: "Now God's home is with human beings! He will live with them, and they shall be his people. God himself will be with them, and he will be their God.[4]

It's not just *our* home that will be on the new earth. God is coming to live there too. He brings heaven down to earth. He plans to fulfil all that's begun to be true for Christians. By his Spirit, God's already living with us. But on the new earth the union and togetherness will be complete.

> He will wipe away all tears from their eyes. There will be no more death, no more grief or crying or pain. The old things have disappeared."[5]

All the suffering and frustration and disappointment of life as we know it on the old earth will be done away. Imperfection will fade into perfection.

> Nothing that is under God's curse will be found in the city. The throne of God and of the Lamb will be in the city, and his servants will worship him.[6]

We shall be finally free of all sin and evil. Free to dedicate ourselves wholly to serving God and Jesus. Some people talk excitedly about the 'new age'. The *real* New Age will of course be this new world of God's at the end of time.

WHAT WILL WE DO?
Work!

> There shall be no more night, and they will not need lamps or sunlight, because the Lord God will be their light, and they will rule as kings for ever and ever.[7]

John doesn't say we'll merely dress or feast like kings; we're to *rule* as kings. We shall have responsibility under God's Lordship for governing the new earth, just as the human race had God-given responsibility for ruling the old earth.[8] We'll be fit, energetic and strong.

Nothing could be further from the traditional cartoons of people floating round on clouds twanging the occasional note on a harp! (Indeed, my chaplain when I was a student said that was nearer his idea of hell!) There'll be plenty for everyone to do. Enough for people of every degree of ambition and energy. There'll be as much as there is on earth now (if not more). Eternity sounds a long time, but we shan't grow tired of it.

WILL WE RECOGNISE EACH OTHER?

God hasn't told us, so we can only guess; but it's hard to imagine we won't recognise each other. When Jesus reappeared to the disciples after coming back to life, his body was perhaps like what ours will be in the next life. He wasn't instantly recognisable. He'd changed in some way. But they soon knew it was him.[9]

What about meeting our loved ones again? Jesus said something rather mysterious.

> For when the dead rise to life, they will be like the angels in heaven and will not marry.[10]

We don't know exactly what he means. We don't know what the angels do instead of marrying! But it's hard to imagine people being *less* closely united than they are on the old earth. Perhaps we'll enjoy with *everyone* the sort of caring and sharing we can only manage with one partner in this life.

But as I say, this is only guesswork. What God has thought important to include in the Bible is the fact that we'll *all* be married — to Jesus!

> Husbands, love your wives just as Christ loved the church and gave his life for it. He did this to dedicate the church to God by his word, after making it clean by washing it in water, in order to present the church to himself in all its beauty — pure and faultless, without spot or wrinkle or any other imperfection.[11]

Perhaps all our attention in the next life — all our love, energy, wonder and excitement — will be taken up with Jesus. He'll be all we need.

---

1   I owe my understanding of the new earth to David Lawrence's exciting book *Heaven ... it's not the end of the world!* (Scripture Union, 1995).
2   Revelation 21:1.
3   Revelation 21:2.
4   Revelation 21:3.
5   Revelation 21:4.
6   Revelation 22:3. Jesus is pictured as 'the Lamb'. By dying on the cross, he made the sacrifice for our sins which lambs in the Old Testament had been a picture of.
7   Revelation 22:5.
8   Genesis 1:26,28.
9   Luke 24:36-43.
10   Mark 12:25.
11   Ephesians 5:25-27.

7.4 "Won't everyone go to heaven?"[1]

I wish I could say that everyone is part of God's plans for the next life.

It's a dreadful thought that anyone could miss out on eternal life in God's presence. It's especially painful when someone's just died — perhaps a friend of yours or a member of your family — and you don't know whether they were a Christian or not. The funeral service talks as if they were. But we can't be sure of the comfort and promises it offers if the dead person wasn't a Christian.

Jesus gave a chilling warning that some people will try to charm or bluff their way into God's kingdom, but they won't succeed.

> Not everyone who calls me 'Lord, Lord' will enter the Kingdom of heaven, but only those who do what my Father in heaven wants them to do. When Judgement Day comes, many will say to me, 'Lord, Lord! In your name we spoke God's message, by your name we drove out many demons and performed many miracles!' Then I will say to them, 'I never knew you. Get away from me, you wicked people!'[2]

Nobody wants to believe him. It's totally out of fashion today to think, let alone teach, that anyone might be excluded. People say, "Jesus would never shut anyone out. Not if they've been sincere. After all, everyone has some good in them."

All of which shows they haven't understood the Christian Good News.

NO-ONE DESERVES TO GET THROUGH

Receiving eternal life is nothing to do with being sincere or good. None of us could ever be good or sincere enough. God is infinitely, blazingly, terrifyingly good. Only if we were totally perfect could we enter his presence.

In our imperfect, polluted state we'd be burnt up. We'd be like a soiled swab or used hypodermic in an operating theatre. Even if we've tried to be sincere about believing in God, or if we've lots of other good points, we're still what Jesus calls "wicked people" inside. And we know it. We wouldn't stand a chance close up to God. It's a kindness not to let us try.

There's only one way to be fit to approach him. That's to have our sins taken away by Jesus' death. Then to have Jesus give us his own 100% perfect record as our passport into God's presence.

> Christ was without sin, but for our sake God made him share our sin in order that in union with him we might share the righteousness of God.[3]

Jesus' death was 'big enough' and complete enough to cover the sins of everybody in the world. But only Christians have accepted his gift of forgiveness and acquittal. So only Christians can be sure of a place in the next life.

WHAT ABOUT PEOPLE WHO AREN'T CHRISTIANS?

People who've deliberately refused to become Christians in this life can't claim to be surprised if they don't make it to the next. They've spent their lives telling Jesus to "get away from us". OK then. He won't force them in against their will. He respects their wishes. He gives them what they've asked for and says, "Get away from **me**."

People who assume they're Christians because they've been brought up to believe in Jesus are a different case. And so are those who've never heard the Christian Good News — and those who've heard it but not understood. Paul describes their position on God's Judgment Day.

> Their conduct shows that what the Law commands is written in their hearts. Their consciences also show that this is true, since their thoughts sometimes accuse them and sometimes defend them.[4]

He seems to leave open the possibility there will be people in the new world who weren't Christians (as we usually use the word) in the old world. Thank God it's not up to us to decide who'll get in. It's up to him. Only he knows the true state of everyone's attitude towards him.

We can rely on the totally just Judge to be fair. He won't condemn people for failing to do things they never knew they had to do. He'll judge them according to the standards they did know about. When their conscience defends them, he'll hear and consider that defence. There will be people whose heart's prayer in life — or even at the very end of it — has been, "God forgive me, because I've done wrong". We can be sure he'll hear and answer that prayer, even if they haven't heard the Good News.

But I wouldn't want to leave things to chance or to the last minute myself. I know if I faced the Day of Judgement on my own merits, my conscience would have to accuse me a great deal more than it could defend me. As soon as I heard Jesus could offer me forgiveness and a new start in life, I knew I had to ask him for it at once.

That's why I want everyone to hear about him. And I pray they'll then become Christians. This is just how people from other religions feel when they become Christians. They want all their old friends to join them. Only that way can we be sure they'll receive eternal life.

1 This is how the question is usually asked. People have been led to believe that Christians 'go to heaven' when they die and live there for ever. See 7.3 "What will heaven be like?" (page 170) for why I think our future really lies on a new earth.

2 Matthew 7:21-23.
3 2 Corinthians 5:21.
4 Romans 2:15.

Why *not*?

When they were younger my son and daughter were forever calling out for judgment — for the other one, of course! If they sensed the faintest sniff of me letting the other one off too lightly, there were howls of "Unfair"!

Children have an instinctive sense of injustice. It only becomes dimmed as we grow older because we get used to having our own way — and to getting away with it.

Deep down, though, human beings want to know the universe is a just place. We want good to be noticed and get its fair reward. And we want evil to be punished and put right. Just think how people who've been wrongly jailed cry out for justice.

GOD IS JUDGE[1]

The Bible insists that God's a Judge who will set the record straight. That's good news.

Except that we've all got bad marks on our record. That's why we secretly hope and kid ourselves it won't happen.

We know we've blown it time and again. But no thunderbolt has struck us down. So perhaps God didn't notice ... or doesn't care ... or isn't there. We mistake his incredible patience for non-existence or softness.

A woman once said to me, "I'm sure God won't punish us for our sins."

"What makes you so sure?" I asked.

"Well, I can't believe Jesus would do a thing like that."

It's so easy to make up a Jesus to fit our own fantasies. The real Jesus said,

> Whatever is now covered up will be uncovered, and every secret will be made known ... Do not be afraid of those who kill the body but cannot kill the soul; rather be afraid of God, who can destroy both body and soul in hell.[2]

> You can be sure that on Judgement Day everyone will have to give account of every useless word he has ever spoken. Your words will be used to judge you — to declare you either innocent or guilty.[3]

He was quite clear there'll be a final day of Judgment. It won't be possible to put God off for ever. One day he'll call us to account for the way we've lived.

But you don't have to wait till then to know what the verdict will be. John says you can see God's judgment on people already in how they react to the light of Jesus.

> This is how the judgment works: the light has come into the world, but people love the darkness rather than the light, because their deeds are evil. All those who do evil things hate the light and will not come to the light, because they do not want their evil deeds to be shown up.[4]

This is one reason why so many people

are embarrassed to talk about Christianity. Their conscience accuses them of wrongdoing. They already know they're in the wrong with God. When he says so on the Day of Judgment, they'll only be able to agree with him. They won't be surprised or aggrieved. They'll already be turning and running from the light. They won't be able to look God in the face.

NO JUDGMENT FOR CHRISTIANS?

What's so different about Christians? We've all thought, said and done things we're ashamed of. We all deserve the sentence 'Guilty' in God's court.

Yet Jesus says,

> I am telling you the truth: those who hear my words and believe in him who sent me have eternal life. They will not be judged, but have already passed from death to life.[5]

The only explanation is that Jesus took our punishment in our place. On the cross he suffered the death penalty our wrongdoings deserved. In his total justice, God condemned our wrongdoing. In his infinite love for us, he provided a completely fair way to save us from the judgment. Fair, but at immense cost to himself.

Christians have gratefully said yes to this unexpected and undeserved rescue act. But anyone who turns their back on it is saying they'd rather face God's death penalty themselves. Brave — but tragic.

DO WHAT WE LIKE?

So if Christians have bypassed the Day of Judgment, can we do what we like from now on, scot-free?[6]

Hold on a moment! Jesus has indeed rescued Christians from dying for our sins on Judgment Day. But that doesn't mean we won't be judged at all.

Jesus told two stories about servants left to trade while their master's away.[7] When he returns he asks for an account of how they've used their investment. In both cases those who've followed his instructions and put the money to good use earn his praise and his reward.

Jesus will treat his Christian servants in the same way. He expects us to show him when he returns how we've used the life and the gifts he gave us. Our place in the next world isn't in doubt. But the exact nature of our work there may be. We can only expect to hear Jesus say "Well done; you're in line for promotion" if we've used our time, talents and money to serve him. How sad if we've wasted them all on ourselves.

Let's go for it. I want to be able to look him in the eye and see he's pleased.

> 'Well done, you good and faithful servant! ... You have been faithful in managing small amounts, so I will put you in charge of large amounts. Come on in and share my happiness!'[8]

---

1 For more on this truth that God will judge the human race, see 3.9 "Why did God need to send his Son to die for us?" (page 77).

2 Matthew 10:26,28.

3 Matthew 12:36,37.

4 John 3:19,20.

5 John 5:24.

6 For another part of the answer to this question, see 3.10 "If we're forgiven by God, can we continue to do what's wrong?" (page 79).

7 Often known as 'the talents' (Matthew 25:14-30) and 'the pounds' (Luke 19:11-27).

8 Matthew 25:21.

7.6 "Heaven and hell aren't real places."

The first Russian astronauts in the early 1960s announced delightedly that they'd been above the earth's atmosphere, but heaven wasn't there. This bolstered their then Government's official atheism.

If they thought Christians would be upset by this, they must have been disappointed. Christians have never believed heaven and hell to be *geographical* places in the universe, which you can plot on a map.

But that doesn't make them unreal or imaginary. They're realities beyond time and space. They're beyond scientific investigation because they're beyond the experience of this life.

They may sound like fairy-tale places. But we believe in them because Jesus taught about them as realities. And as he said himself, he ought to know!

> ... no one has ever gone up to heaven except the Son of Man, who came down from heaven.[1]

Heaven was his home.

HEAVEN

Jesus taught about heaven in 51 separate recorded remarks. The commonest thing he said is that God lives there. It's the place of perfect justice and peace.

In a sense it can be our home too. Not in the future after we've died — God's people will then be living on the new earth. But right now, we can be citizens of heaven as much as we are of earth.[2]

This is the second commonest thing Jesus said about heaven. 33 times in Matthew's Gospel Jesus refers to "the kingdom of heaven" (in other places he calls it the kingdom of God). He uses the phrase to describe life under God's kingship, which begins for Christians here on earth. The heart of heaven isn't future bliss, but being with God and Jesus.

Through the presence of the Holy Spirit in our lives, we're *already* at home with God. The life and rules of heaven start operating in our lives now.

HELL

Hell's the opposite of heaven. It's not Jesus' home. It's the sphere of existence he's totally absent from. Because it has no touch of his blessing it lacks any redeeming features. That's why Jesus sometimes called it "the darkness"[3].

He also called it "the fire that never goes out"[4]. In his parable of the Rich Man and Lazarus, the Rich Man goes to Hades (another name for hell) and complains, "I am in great pain in this fire"[5]. This led to gruesomely literal paintings and preaching in the Middle Ages. I hope and think the idea's more spiritual than physical.

The Bible has to use pictorial images to paint the future; we can't yet understand every detail. For instance, one of the ways it describes the next life for Christians is calling the Church Jesus' bride.[6] We can have *ideas* about what this'll be like, but I'm sure the reality will turn out beyond our wildest dreams!

Hell-fire seems to me to describe the devastating judgment of God on a human life that has deliberately defied or ignored him. Perhaps too the burning, gnawing regret of a conscience that realises it's lost its chance to get right with God. It dwells on the wrong things the person did, the wrong turnings they took. All the reasons why hell is indeed the right place for them to land up. And it does so for ever.

There have been two popular ideas to try to soften this awful starkness in Jesus' teaching. One is sometimes called 'purgatory'. The idea is that the fire he describes is (at least for some people) a refining fire as in metal-making. It gradually burns the dross or wrong things out of them. And eventually they are purified and ready to enter heaven.

It's a comforting idea. But it has no basis in the Bible. So we can build no hopes on it at all.

It arose because people couldn't bear to accept what the Bible says about God. They often say, "I can't believe a loving God would send anyone to hell". They forget that he's holy and just as well as loving. Moses claimed to be passing on God's own words when he gave this warning.

> If you ... worship other gods, the
> LORD's anger will come against you
> like fire and will destroy you
> completely, because the LORD your
> God, who is present with you,
> tolerates no rivals.[7]

Some people think they can dismiss these ideas because they come in the Old Testament. But the New Testament confirms them: "our God is indeed a destroying fire".[8]

This talk of God destroying leads to the second attempt to tone down the idea of hell. It's sometimes called 'annihilation'. It suggests that while the future for God's people is *conscious* eternal life, hell is *unconscious* eternal death. People who 'go to hell' simply cease to exist. They're destroyed — lost and gone for ever — and they know nothing more about it.

This is a sad enough fate in all conscience. But it's not the natural meaning of Jesus' words. I wouldn't want to build any hopes on it. Jesus appears to teach that God's "destroying fire" never burns out.[9] And Revelation warns that "The smoke of the fire that torments them goes up for ever and ever. There is no relief day or night for those who worship the beast ... "[10]

The main point is that Jesus talked about hell as if it exists. And as God the Son he should know. He referred to it by name ten times in his recorded teaching —not to mention the times he called it other names like fire or darkness. That's over twice as often as Paul, who some people imagine was more of a 'hellfire' preacher than Jesus.

But heaven and hell aren't just a couple of words to count and haggle over. According to Jesus, every one of us will spend eternity in one place or the other, with God or without him. How important to make sure we're in the right one!

One of Jesus' clearest warnings:

> Go in through the narrow gate,
> because the gate to hell is wide
> and the road that leads to it is easy,
> and there are many who travel it.
> But the gate to life is narrow and the
> way that leads to it is hard, and there
> are few people who find it.[11]

1   John 3:13.
2   Philippians 3:20. For more about our future destiny being a new earth rather than heaven, see 7.3 "What will heaven be like?" (page 170).
3   Matthew 8:12; 25:30.
4   Mark 9:43.
5   Luke 16:24.
6   2 Corinthians 11:2; Ephesians 5:25-27,31,32. We gather that the idea must be highly symbolic from Revelation 21:2 which compares the heavenly *city* to a "bride dressed to meet her husband". For a few first thoughts on what this idea means, go to 7.3 "What will heaven be like?" (page 170).
7   Deuteronomy 6:15.
8   Hebrews 12:29.
9   Mark 9:43-48. Compare God's appearance to Moses as a flame in a bush that was "on fire but not burning up" (Exodus 3:2).
10 Revelation 14:11. "Worshipping the beast" is Revelation's symbolic language for *not* worshipping Jesus. For more on the beast, go to 7.9 "Won't there be signs that it's nearly the end of the world?" (page 182).
11 Matthew 7:13,14.

7.7 "What does the Bible say about the end of the world?"

The 20th century was the first when the end of the world seemed really likely.

In previous centuries, when people understood far less about how the world works — and how easily it could be destroyed — it was hard to imagine how anything seeming so solid and resourceful could come to an end.

But now we know about nuclear bombs ... viruses spreading faster than we can devise inoculation or antidote ... loss of the protective ozone layer ... destruction of the environment and waste of vital resources.

Serious thinkers wonder how far into the 21st century the world can survive. We may well be the final generation.

GOD GOT THERE FIRST

People talk about the world's dwindling chances of surviving as if it threatens our Christian belief in God. They presumably think that *we* think he's under some obligation to keep the world going.

He isn't. The New Testament insists repeatedly that God will bring the present world order to an end. Suddenly and spectacularly.

Jesus taught:

> The coming of the Son of Man will be like what happened in the time of Noah. In the days before the flood people ate and drank, men and women married, up to the very day Noah went into the boat; yet they did not realize what was happening until the flood came and swept them all away. That is how it will be when the Son of Man comes.[1]

Peter wrote:

> ... by ... the water of the flood ... the old world was destroyed. But the heavens and the earth that now exist are being preserved by the same command of God, in order to be destroyed by fire. They are being kept for the day when godless people will be judged and destroyed ... On that Day the heavens will disappear with a shrill noise, the heavenly bodies will burn up and be destroyed, and the earth with everything in it will vanish.[2]

All previous generations found it hard to see how these scenes could happen unless or until God chucked a bomb into the works. To us they're all too frighteningly possible as a natural consequence of processes we've triggered ourselves. They could accompany any of the doomsday scenarios people have sketched for us —nuclear holocaust, lethal sunrays, ecological collapse.

God's in charge. He could use any of these nightmares — or none of them — as the cue to bring the world to an end. He has his own plan and timetable.

GOD SAYS IT'S GOOD NEWS

The end of the world's only part of God's script. The difference between him and the prophets of doom is that for them the end of the world's the end of everything. For God it's when he at last gets things back to how he wants them.

He plans a new earth which will be perfect and never come to an end.[3]

"Pie in the sky," laugh the scoffers.

But he predicted a violent end to the present world, long before it looked likely.

If events now prove him right in that first part of his plan, why should he be wrong in the second part?

1   Matthew 24:37-39.
2   2 Peter 3:6-7,10. This is, of course, not the whole story. The old world will come to an end like this to make way for the new (Revelation 21:1). Paul's description of the process in Romans 8:18-23 also concentrates on the end result.
3   Revelation 21:1-7. See also 7.3 "What will heaven be like?" (page 170).

7.8 "Will Jesus really come back? If so, when?"

Many people think Jesus and the early Christians expected him to come back to earth within a few years. They think his failure to do so means Christianity isn't true. They say things like, "2000 years is a bit of a long time. You can't expect us still to believe Jesus will come back."

They don't realise the New Testament foresaw them — and how to answer them.

> They will mock you and will ask, "He promised to come, didn't he? Where is he? Our ancestors have already died, but everything is still the same as it was since the creation of the world!" ... But do not forget one thing, my dear friends! There is no difference in the Lord's sight between one day and a thousand years; to him the two are the same. The Lord is not slow to do what he has promised, as some think. Instead, he is patient with you, because he does not want anyone to be destroyed, but wants all to turn away from their sins.[1]

2000 years is *not* a long time to God — especially if we're using it to bring people the Good News about Jesus. To him it's not even a long weekend.

WHEN?

In any case, Jesus never said he'd come back soon. He said the waiting period would be "a long time".[2]

As for the actual date, he admitted frankly this was one thing he didn't know.

> No one knows ... when that day or hour will come — neither the angels in heaven, nor the Son [i.e. Jesus himself]; only the Father knows.[3]

This hasn't, of course, stopped Jehovah's Witnesses and various other groups trying to predict the date of the end of the world.[4] Only to be left with egg on their faces.

The true teaching of Jesus and the New Testament can be summed up like this: he must come one day — he may come any day — so be ready for him!

God knows that being ready for Jesus to come back at any moment is the best way to keep us on our toes. It would have done the early Christians no good at all if he'd told them Jesus wasn't coming for at least 2000 years! They'd have been badly depressed. And many of them would have slackened off spiritually.

The Old Testament contains more prophecies of Jesus' second coming than of his first. It more often sees the Messiah as a mighty judge at the end of time than as a baby in a feed-trough.[5] Yet it got the first coming absolutely right. So isn't it even more likely to be right about Jesus' return?

HOW AND WHY?

The contrast between Jesus' first and second comings throws more light on why Christians are so sure he'll come back. He has unfinished business to see to.

He came weak, as a baby in a poor family. He will come strong, as Lord of the whole universe.

He came quietly, virtually unnoticed. He will come with a trumpet fanfare no-one can miss.

He came to be part of the world as it was, and still is. He will come to bring it to an end, and make a new one.

He came to sow the seeds of a new kingdom in people's lives. He will come when the harvest is full-grown; it's the only kingdom that will survive, and he'll be its King.

He came to suffer. He will come to be in charge, and bring all suffering to an end.

He came to endure an unjust trial which bent the rules. He will come to judge the whole human race with perfect fairness.

He must come one day — he may come any day — so be ready.

Look, he is coming on the clouds! Everyone will see him, including those who pierced him. All peoples on earth will mourn over him. So shall it be![6]

When the Son of Man comes as King and all the angels with him, he will sit on his royal throne, and the people of all the nations will be gathered before him. Then he will divide them into two groups, just as a shepherd separates the sheep from the goats.[7]

Be on watch, be alert, for you do not know when the time will come.[8]

1 2 Peter 3:3,4,8,9.
2 Matthew 25:19.
3 Mark 13:32.
4 For more about Jehovah's Witnesses and other sub-Christian sects, go to 6.9 "What's heresy?" (page 161).
5 E.g. 2 Samuel 7:16; Psalm 2:7,8; 45:6,7; 93:10-13; 110:1-4; Isaiah 9:7; 11:1-9; 35:5-10; Daniel 7:13,14.
6 Revelation 1:7.
7 Matthew 25:31,32.
8 Mark 13:33.

7.9 "Won't there be signs that it's nearly the end of the world?"

A preacher asked each of the elders who met him to pray just before the service, "Are you expecting Jesus to come back tonight?" One by one they said, "Well, no." "Not really." "Not tonight." Then he told them, "The text for my sermon is, 'the Son of Man will come at an hour when you are not expecting him' ".[1]

My minister once tried it on me and his other assistant. "Do you think Jesus could come tonight?" "Yes," I said piously, "I certainly do."

But my colleague said, "No. I think things have got to get a lot worse before he comes." What did she mean?

WARNING SIGNS?

There are certain passages in the New Testament which have led many Christians to expect a number of earth-shaking events before the end comes. Some come in Jesus' teaching.

> Be on guard, and don't let anyone deceive you. Many men, claiming to speak for me, will come and say, 'I am he!' and they will deceive many people. And don't be troubled when you hear the noise of battles close by and news of battles far away.[2]

But it's wrong to call these signs of the end approaching. For Jesus went on:

> Such things must happen, *but they do not mean that the end has come.* Countries will fight each other; kingdoms will attack one another. There will be earthquakes everywhere, and there will be famines. These things are like the first pains of childbirth.[3]

First pains, not last! They're not signs that the world is about to end. They're typical conditions of the whole period between Jesus' first coming and his second.

THE LAST DAYS?

Part of the confusion comes from a common expression in the New Testament. Jesus and the other writers often refer to "the last days" or "in those days". It's natural to imagine they mean the final countdown to Jesus' return.

But in fact they mean the whole of the last stage or era of world history. We're in 'the last days' now and have been ever since the New Testament was written. The period stretches from the last but one great event in God's plan for the world — the coming of the Holy Spirit on the Day of Pentecost — till the end.

This has helped me decide what I think about five words and events connected with Jesus' Second Coming. Different Christians understand them in different ways.[4] But many think they'll appear or happen shortly before the end.

- 1. MILLENNIUM. Not in this case the year 2000! The word millennium means a thousand years. In this connection it refers to Revelation 20:1-6, which says Jesus will reign for a thousand years before the end, with those who've been martyred for him.

- 2. RAPTURE. This word means being taken away. It refers to Matthew 24:40,41 where some people are taken when Jesus returns, while others are left.

- 3. TRIBULATION. This is another word for suffering. It's often applied to the special sufferings of Christians in the final death-throes before the end of the world.

- 4. ARMAGEDDON. This is the place where, according to Revelation 16:14,16, "all the kings of the world" will gather for a final battle "on the great Day of Almighty God".
- 5. ANTICHRIST. This name's applied to a shadowy figure in the New Testament, who's the spearhead of opposition to Jesus. In 2 Thessalonians there's a "Wicked One", and in Revelation a "Beast". These may or may not be meant to be the same person.

But John, who uses the name "AntiChrist", makes clear that in his view this enemy isn't just one figure at the end of time. It's all opponents of Jesus in these last days and hours.

> Dear children, this is the last hour; and as you have heard that the antichrist is coming, even now many antichrists have come. This is how we know it is the last hour ... Who is the liar? It is the man who denies that Jesus is the Christ. Such a man is the antichrist — he denies the Father and the Son.[5]

So in the same way I take 'tribulation' to be a word for the persecution which Christians endure throughout the last days. And I see the 'millennium' as a symbolic vision of the whole last age. As we know, it's lasted well over a thousand years. But most of the numbers in Revelation are symbolic rather than exact.

As for the 'rapture' of Christians who are still alive on earth, I expect that to happen when Jesus comes back to bring the world to an end — not before or after. This fits in well with the rest of what the New Testament says.[6]

The battle of Armageddon comes in a chapter describing God's final judgment on everyone in the world who has opposed him. It appears to me as another symbolic picture of the end of the world. The name Armageddon means 'mountain of Megiddo'; it's a place in Israel which has witnessed many important battles in history, and so is a natural symbolic name to fit in with the rest of Revelation.

These are of course only my understanding of the New Testament. Don't just take my word for it, but reach your own opinion on what the Bible teaches.

On my understanding, though, we shan't get any more warnings about the end of the world than we've had already. It could happen any time.

---

1 Matthew 24:44.
2 Mark 13:5-7. I don't actually think Jesus is talking here about the end of the world at all. He is answering the disciples' question, "Tell us when this will be" (verse 4); they are referring to his prophecy of the end of the *Jerusalem temple* (verses 1-2). This simply reinforces my point that these outbreaks of religious, political and environmental turmoil are *not* signs that the world is about to end.
3 Mark 13:7,8.
4 And some talk about them more often than I think their rather rare appearances in the New Testament really deserve.
5 1 John 2:18,22 New International Version. Good News Bible translates AntiChrist as "Enemy of Christ".
6 Compare the parallel teaching in 1 Thessalonians 4:16,17, which seems clearly to be talking about the end of the world.

7.10 "Why all this morbid talk about dying and the end of the world? Life is for living *now*."

True, but —

YOU DON'T KNOW HOW LONG YOU'VE GOT

A visiting speaker at our school amazed us by saying, "Statistics show that a quarter of you will be dead before you're 40."

I've no idea whether he's turned out to be right with our lot. But one thing's certainly true: we don't know when we'll die —or when Jesus will come back.

Yet we *do* know for absolute certain that our lives will come to an end one way or the other. A bit stupid not to be ready.

Jesus told a story about a man like that. Rich and getting richer. He'd got everything he wanted out of life. "Lucky man!" he said to himself. "Take life easy, eat, drink, and enjoy yourself!" He could be the star of any TV commercial.

But God said, "You fool! This very night you will have to give up your life".

Punctured, burst, gone. Nothing left. Just an empty space where a man once was. And a handful of ash from the crematorium.

And a label on the ash container asking the question God's asking you, "Who will get all these things you have kept for yourself?"[1]

Set your heart on a good time in this life, and it'll slip through your fingers. But look at this life as a training for the next, and you'll get the best out of it.

YOU DO KNOW WHERE YOU'RE GOING

Some Christians have earned the description, 'so heavenly minded they're no earthly use'. But that shouldn't stop you keeping heaven in your sights. In fact, it's the people with their eyes on the next life who make the most of this one. After all, you drive much better if you know where you're going.

What does it mean for Christians to 'keep heaven in their sights'? Jesus told another story to make it clear.

> It will be like a man who goes away from home on a journey and leaves his servants in charge, after giving to each one his own work to do and after telling the doorkeeper to keep watch.[2]

Work — and watch. We each have our work to do. Job or studies — family duties —church commitments — voluntary work —other forms of Christian service — get on and do them. Do them well. Make them count.

And all the time, keep watching. Listen out for Jesus' car parking outside, his footsteps on the path, his key in the door … That's the moment we're waiting for. That's when our work will find its true reward.

> Be on guard, then, because you do not know when the master of the house is coming — it might be in the evening or at midnight or before dawn or at sunrise. If he comes suddenly, he must not find you asleep. What I say to you, then, I say to all: *Watch!*[3]

If we *knew* Jesus was coming in the next 24 hours, what difference would it make? I know I'd change all my plans and do a massive sort-out. Put the really important things right in time for him to see.

Wouldn't it be great if we didn't need to change anything at all? We could just get on with the work he's given us because all the important things were already right.

Hmmmm. I need to think about that. Before it's too late.

> You have been raised to life with Christ, so set your hearts on the things that are in heaven, where Christ sits at the right-hand side of God. Keep your minds fixed on things there, not on things here on earth. For you have died, and your life is hidden with Christ in God. Your real life is Christ and when he appears, then you will appear with him and share his glory![4]

1. What would you want to say to comfort (a) a Christian afraid of dying; (b) someone with no faith whose closest friend or relation has just died?
2. How would you answer someone who says, "It's arrogant to say you know you will go to heaven"?
3. How would you answer someone who says, "A God who would send people to hell is a cruel sadist"?
4. How would you answer someone who says, "Things are getting better, or at least they will get steadily better, in the New Age"?
5. What would you do today if you knew Jesus was coming back tomorrow?
6. What do you see as the pluses and minuses if you die or Jesus comes back before you reach (a) middle age; (b) old age?

1   Luke 12:16-20.
2   Mark 13:34.
3   Mark 13:35-37.
4   Colossians 3:1-4.

A Window To Heaven

Dr Diane M. Komp

What would you do as a hospital doctor when children facing death—or their parents—witness to you about faith? The official line is not to get involved, to stay 'professional'. But that was not Dr Komp's reaction …

'I have met people who claim they lost their faith over the agonising question, How can a loving God let innocent children die? Dr Komp is the first person I've met who found a personal faith while treating such dying children. Her story —and theirs— deserves our attention'.
Philip Yancey
Author of *Disappointment with God*

'Unforgettably inspiring'
Sandy Millar, Holy Trinity Brompton

'Out of harrowing experiences while looking after children with cancer, Diane Komp, a paediatric oncologist of international repute, draws conclusions about the human condition that should make us pause and think …
I read it with a lump in my throat.'
J.S. Malpas D.Phil., FRCP, FRCR, FFPM
St Bartholomew's Hospital, London
ISBN 1-897913-32-X
Highland Books   Price £3.99